THE EMERGING RIGHTS OF CHILDREN IN TREATMENT FOR MENTAL AND CATASTROPHIC ILLNESSES

Frank H. Marsh

University Press of America™

Library of Congress Catalog Card Number: 79-66481

TO MY WIFE, MARTY,
with many thanks for everything

CONTENTS

"Like the imbecile, the crazed, and the beast, over children there is no law."

Thomas Hobbes, *Leviathan*, Volume 3.

"Neither the Fourteenth Amendment nor the Bill of Rights is for adults alone."

Supreme Court, *In Re Gault*.

ACKNOWLEDGMENTS

I am indebted to many people, and to three institutions for help with this book. Much of this book was written during the academic year 1977-78 at the University of Tennessee when, due to the generous support of the Institute on Human Values in Medicine, I was able to engage in significant research on the rights of children in medicine.

Glen Graber, John Davis, L.B. Cebik, and Rem Edwards, all of the University of Tennessee, read the whole of early drafts and helped me enormously with their comments. Professor Graber, in particular, read and reread my manuscript many times, and stimulated me to make major improvements throughout it, especially the two chapters on ethical rights.

I am also indebted to my colleagues at Old Dominion University for making the necessary time and funds available for completion of this book. Lastly, I am grateful to my wife, Marty, and Susan Sasser for their seemly endless task of proof reading and indexing the final draft.

CHAPTER 1

INTRODUCTION
AND
GENERAL CONSIDERATIONS

The purpose of this work is a comprehensive examination of the legal and ethical rights of children in treatment for mental and catastrophic illnesses. While there is some general literature dealing with children's rights, it is comprised for the most part of independent essays which are mostly unrelated to one another. There are several excellent studies on children's rights in the areas of education, domestic relations, and juvenile court procedures; however, there is no exacting study that pulls together a comparative analysis of existing legal rights with purported ethical rights of children in treatment for mental or catastrophic illnesses.

It should be noted that the term "rights in treatment" has been employed rather than "right to treatment." The terms have different meanings. The initial right of a person to medical treatment or health care is in itself a far-reaching legal and ethical issue. For example, it has been asked: Does every child have a right to some type of psychiatric health care? The "right to treatment" will not be discussed here in the general sense of a moral claim to health care. I will be concerned only with the constellation of legal and ethical rights that surround a child once he or she has been admitted to treatment; when he or she actually is in treatment for a mental illness or catastrophic disease and is receiving or is about to receive treatment for his or her malady.

If we picture the issue of children's rights as making up an extended continuum, we will see at one extremity the advocates of an historical status quo — absolute parental control, while at the other end are the

1

proponents of an equality of children's rights with those rights normally assigned to adults. From an examination of legal rights of children, with their historical base, the law will be seen to be floating, perhaps unbelievably and incongruously at times, from one end of the continuum towards the other and back again.

This work then is, first of all, an inquiry into the existing legal rights of children in treatment for mental and catastrophic illnesses. From an historical perspective and a study of current law, we will be able to see that the legal theory behind children's rights is changing and determine to some extent the general direction in which this change is headed and perhaps how far it should take us.

Secondly, because ethical rights generally precede legal rights, we will examine within a general framework of ethics, specific rights of children and consider where they support existing law and where they do not, and, where there is a purported ethical right without legal support.

I have divided my discussion into three parts. Chapter 2 begins with a general history of children's rights which lead up to the initial recognition by the Supreme Court of the United States that the protection of the Constitution extends to minors.[1]

Chapters 3 and 4 are directed to physical illnesses, and Chapters 5 and 6 to mental illnesses. In these four chapters, some specific legal and ethical questions will be raised along with corresponding arguments for an answer to these questions. Before proceeding, and for clarity and reference, I have provided the following definitions of various terms and phrases that will be employed throughout the essay.

1. A minor — A minor is a person who has not reached his or her eighteenth birthday and has not been legally emancipated. The terms "child" and "minor" are interchangeable and carry the same meaning.

2. Catastrophic illness—Generally a catastrophic illness can be classified as any illness that requires long-term hospitalization of the patient and/or a radical course of treatment such as major surgery, chemotherapy, radiation, hemodialysis, etc. In almost every instance, the threat of death to the patient, or a serious residual disability from the illness prevails. Examples of catastrophic illnesses are: cancer, nephritis (with failure of kidneys), cardiovascular disease, cerebrovascular accident. I have also decided to include within this category those accidents to children which are of catastrophic proportions, such as high cervical cord lesion with resulting paraplegia. The legal and ethical issues and rights in such situations are no less than those found in medically prescribed treatments for osteosarcoma in children. With the inclusion of catastrophic accidents, we will embrace in our inquiry, the whole area of children's rights within the matter of substantial or major medical care.

2

3. Mental Illness — Children in treatment for mental illnesses include: all children who have been committed or are in the process of being committed to a mental hospital for treatment or custody either voluntarily by parents or guardian, involuntarily by parents or guardian, involuntarily by court commitment under parens patriae, or through juvenile court commitment in exercise of state police powers.

4. Rights — legal and moral. For the purpose of my essay, a legal right is a claim whose enforcement is based either upon the constitution, statutes, or the common law. In the context of my discussion, these claim-rights will be referred to as constitutional rights, statutory rights, and common law rights. A legal right is at most prima facie.

To have a moral right to anything is, in short, to have a very strong moral claim upon it. It is the strongest kind of claim there is.[2] If we say that a minor has a moral right to do "X", we are saying that he or she has the strongest claim there is to undertake a chosen course of action.

I readily accept the fact that the definition ascribed here to moral rights is not the last word on rights or the only definition applicable to rights. However, nearly all writers do maintain and argue that there is some intimate connection between having a claim and having a right. For the most part, their arguments fall into the following distinctive areas: identifying rights as claims without qualification; defining "right" as a justified or justifiable claim; defining "right" as a recognized claim; and finally defining "right" as a valid claim. The last view that identifies a right as a valid claim is becoming increasingly popular and is supported by such rights theorists as Feinberg, Melden, and Morris.

Under this view, having a claim is very much like the legal phrase "having a prima facie case." As a general rule, a plaintiff in a law suit establishes a prima facie case for imposing liability on the defendant when he establishes the legal grounds that will be sufficient for liability unless overcome by more compelling reasons on behalf of the defendant. For Feinberg, in a parallel prima facie sense of claim, having a claim to do "X" is not the same as having a right to do "X", but is, instead, having a case of at least minimal plausibility that one has a right to "X", a case that does establish a right, not to "X", but to fair consideration. Thus, Feinberg argues that claims differ in degree because some are stronger than others, but that rights do not differ; no one right is more of a right than another.[3] Feinberg, Melden and others believe that this is the important difference between rights and mere claims. "Prima facie" is built into the sense of "claim" but the notion of a "prima facie" right makes little sense.[4] In the end, Feinberg suggests that a man has a moral right when he has a claim the recognition of which is called for — "not (necessarily) by legal rules — but by moral principles, or the principles of an enlightened conscience." Thus, he says, to have a right is to have a claim against someone whose

3

recognition as valid is called for by some set of governing rules or moral principles.

While I do not intend to make my stand in support of children's rights here, there is a problem with Feinberg's complete separation of claim from right that bothers me. The "prima facie sense" of claim does not allow for the establishment of any permanent right. For example, a person may have carried the day with his or her claim, thus establishing a right. However, against another contestant, the right must revert back to the status of a claim which must be validated again before it can be called a right. It would seem that there could never be a world of rights as rights, but only a world of "prima facie" claims. What I suspect though is that the distinction between rights and claims is not as sharp as Feinberg and his supporters suppose to be the case; nor is it necessary to argue so. The use of the word "right" can simply be understood to be the definition of a strong claim. In this sense, a right is always prima facie too, and becomes the predominant right in any given situation when the claim is validated. By understanding the prima facie sense of rights we can accept the position in ethics and law, that the principle upon which a certain right is founded might have to yield to another with which it competes on facts, and that the weight of a right is its power to withstand such competition.

We can have rights then, legal and moral, which will be absolute against certain other rights, and yet subservient in a sense to some other particular right. While I partly agree with Feinberg, it does seem to make a lot of sense, however, to say that rights, especially legal rights, are prima facie in nature. For example, if I have under Feinberg's thesis, validated my claim to ownership of a certain piece of real estate, then I will have an absolute right to this property — that is, that no other person's right to the property is more of a right than mine. However, this is not so. While I may appear to have an absolute right against the world, the state possesses the right to take my property through the principle of imminent domain. Feinberg most certainly would counter here by arguing that my original claim to ownership of the property was validated against everyone except the state, but this doesn't make too much sense. If a claim is validated against one party as a right, how can it not be validated against other parties as well, unless, it maintains a prima facie sense when it becomes a right. Thus, I would offer, the prima facie character of the nature of all rights refers to the objective features of the rights as rights, that there is always the possibility that in a given situation the expression of any one of them may be overridden by more stringent consideration.

In concluding this section I would suggest that we needn't really get hung up on the issue of claim and right, it is enough for our purposes to have a general meaning of "moral right" and "legal right." I believe that other definitions can be employed as well without changing the basic context of what is written and discussed, keeping in mind that the overall thesis is the examination of rights (or claims) of children. What is important is the argument which follows in Chapter 4 establishing the ethical framework that will support certain prima facie rights in children. Also, another important note to remember is that a moral right can exist between a person and an institution as well as between persons. Thus a minor patient can have, for example, a moral right to humane treatment by a mental institution, though obviously, the response to the right is executed by agents of the institution.

CHAPTER 2

THE HISTORICAL PERSPECTIVE
OF CHILDREN'S RIGHTS

For all practical purposes, the history of children's rights did not begin until the nineteenth century. Prior to that time, there is little if any recorded evidence that substantial notice was being paid to the needs of children, or, especially, to the concept of legal and ethical rights as we understand them today.

Even though children historically have always had some rights, they did not possess them in the sense in which we view personhood and personhood-rights today. Whether we speak of natural rights, God-given rights, inalienable rights, constitutional rights, or any source of rights, they were to be possessed only by persons, and a minor was excluded from personhood. Until the magical age of adulthood was attained, as dictated by society, a boy or girl remained a non-entity. If they did possess a right or were granted some politico-social right by law, it was because of an assigned class or status such as a legatee with the right to inherit property. It was easy for society to dismiss any consideration of children's rights simply because children as children did not exist in the eyes of the law.

In looking at the history of children's rights in this chapter, two distinct phases will be noted. (1) The development of an awareness by society of children as a special privileged class that is to remain dependent and (2) a strengthening of parental control of this dependent existence. Many of the critical and unresolved bioethical dilemmas surrounding medical treatment of children today spring from the historical relationship of parent and child.

The concept of children as a distinct group of citizens is unique to modern western culture. While it may be argued ethically that certain rights have always existed though unrecognized, historically it was not until the latter part of the middle ages that a clear concept of childhood emerged. Most languages, in fact, had no word meaning "child."[1]

Prior to the nineteenth century there were no clear-cut rights assigned to an individual by the fact that (considered by our standards today) he or she happened to be a minor. There was no specific class known as or called minors which was the beneficiary of laws or customs. Then, as it is now, in order to have legal rights, subjects of the state had to be considered as persons. Before the middle ages, infant mortality was so high that parents in general refused to become psychologically attached to their children. Until a child reached the age of 7 or 8, he simply was not regarded as a person. If children survived past the age of 7 or 8, they joined adult society and had no unique privileges, no distinctive clothing of institutions.[2] To think about children as persons of unique status is a recent phenomenon.

The absence of childhood can be seen if we look at tenth century art. In the tenth century, artists were unable to depict a child except as a man on a smaller scale. The argument has been presented that because medieval art did not know childhood, or did not attempt to portray it, it seems probable, that there was no place for childhood in the medieval world. For example, in the painting of Gospels of Jesus where He is asking children to come to Him, the miniaturist has grouped eight men around Jesus, only depicting them on a smaller scale. There is evidence that the refusal to accept child morphology in art is to be found also in most ancient civilizations.[3]

Before the enactment of specific statutes of emancipation, such as those that exist in the United States defining adulthood, there was no clear breaking point in age where a person crossed over to adulthood from childhood. Custom for the most part dictated acceptance of a child into the adult world. Generally the idea of childhood was considered simply to be an age of life and was bound up with the idea of dependency. One could leave childhood only by leaving the state of dependence. Historically (and even in modern jargon) words associated with childhood would indicate a man or woman of humble rank, whose submission to others remained absolute. We need only to look at the term "boy" when applied to a 40-year-old black male, or "lost children" when speaking of army troops situated in a precarious position at the battle front. A "petit garcon" was not necessarily a child but a young servant and a Civil War captain might utter to his troops under fire, "Courage children, stand fast."[4]

To be sure, as previously stated, a child even though a non-entity always possessed certain rights legalistically or through custom. The English common law, upon which American common law is rooted, almost from its recorded inception centuries ago recognized two central rights. (1) A child had the right to be born. As the law speaks, "from time immemor-

7

ial" the willful abortion of an unborn child was most reprehensible, if not criminal. And, (2) because a child was deemed to exist from the moment of conception, the right of child *en ventre sa mere* to inherit property was beyond dispute.[5]

The basis of these two rights, however, was not found in the child as a person, but rather in the religious doctrine covering the conception of the soul and its moment of being, and the necessity for an orderly transfer of property. Further, even though the two rights were possessed (that term is debatable) by the child, total control of the child's existence remained at the pleasure of his or her parent. The concept of "person" was distinguished from that of the soul, in that a child became a person only when society accepted him as an adult. Adulthood, as established by society, carried with it personhood and the socio-political rights associated with it. It is a point of interest that only a child born to a valid marriage was accorded the right of inheritance. The child born out of wedlock had no legal relation to the family unit and could not inherit property. In fact, it can be said that the illegitimate child had only the right to be born and not murdered. The law relented later, with the enactment of the "bastard statutes," to permit an illegitimate child to inherit from his mother but continues to the present day the prohibition of any inheritance from the father.[6]

It is documented that the Romans literally gave to fathers the power of life and death over their children.[7] In the eighteenth century under the English common law, the term "children's rights" would have been a nonsequitur. There and elsewhere children were regarded as chattels of the family and wards of the state with only the barest of legal rights. Blackstone, considered to be the father of the common law, wrote very little about children's rights. Instead, he took the opposite tack and stressed the duties of children to their fathers.[8] These duties were unilateral in nature with no counter-duties prevailing from father to child. For example, the obligation to provide sustenance for one's children was not a response to any particular right possessed by the children but was an obligation to the state. This duty to the state or to society emanated from the desire of the state to avoid an accumulation of homeless children on the streets of the cities and in the institutions.

The beginning of the 19th century still found children subject to virtually absolute parental control with little protection and unable to assert any individual claims or rights. While children did receive certain rights, these were received by them in some other legal status and not as persons. Thus a child had a right as a party injured by tortfeasors, not as a child injured by tortfeasors; or, a child inherited property as a legatee not as a child. These rights could only be exercised by children vicariously through adult representation. (This fact is still true today. A minor cannot sue or pursue a claim in court in his or her own name.)

The wide disparity between children's rights and their legal responsibilities should be noted. While possessing no autonomous rights of their own which might correspond to adult rights, children were nevertheless held accountable in the law by adult standards. For example, it is recorded that as late as 1828, a 13-year-old boy was hanged for murder in New Jersey.[9]

Thus, up to the nineteenth century, outside of the two rights previously mentioned, the right to be born and the right to inherit property and the right not to be murdered, a minor remained a non-entity. The concept of children's rights, separate and apart from parental representation was on the horizon though. This concept, however, was to take the position of creating a special class of citizens to be protected by laws with the rights being more in the nature of privileges. The laws that were to fill the books, though perhaps necessary at the time, were based upon the same rationale as the existing laws for women and slaves. Like women, children were still the property of the father and as such, were to remain dependent upon him. It is amazing, but up until the early 1900's only the father could contract, sue and vote. The class known as children along with the class known as women were still to be denied the full concept of personhood.

The basic rationale for depriving people of rights where a dependency relationship exists such as parent-child, is that certain individuals are incapable or undeserving of the right to take care of themselves and consequently they need some type of social institutions to safeguard their positions. Society presumes that under the circumstances what it is doing is the best thing for the individual. The relative powerlessness of children makes them uniquely vulnerable to this rationale. The protecting legislative acts which were enacted beginning in the late nineteenth century, though well intended, were based upon the rationale of dependency and the lack of the right of self-autonomy. This rationale is not without ethical support. Political and ethical theorists from Plato onward have sought to specify property child-rearing practices and have postulated the proper position of children within society.

Hobbes, for example, argued that children are to be cared for solely because they are capable of serving their fathers; children are assigned a position of complete dependence.

"Like the imbecile, the crazed, and the beast, over children there is no law."[10]

Hobbes believed that children possessed no natural rights and likewise, no rights by social contract because they lack the ability to make contracts with other members of society. Children could not understand or fathom the consequences of contracts. Instead, they must acknowledge their father as supreme sovereign.

John Locke assumed a somewhat different position than Hobbes. For Locke, children were to be under the control and jurisdiction of their parents until they were able to make it on their own, a time when they were no longer dependent upon their parents. Until that time, because a child lacks understanding, he or she could not exert his or her will. In Locke's view, children can cast off their dependency only when they become adults and are rational enough to understand the principles by which they are governed. Locke, as others of the time, did not entertain the thought that a 15-year-old boy or girl could be rational enough to comprehend events and circumstances that take place in the adult world. It was presumed as it is today that rationality accompanies the chronological age for attaining adulthood.[11]

Locke did feel, however, that children possessed natural rights which were intrinsic properties in need of protection. In granting this he did not address the critical issue that there might be conflicts between the natural rights of parents and children. This issue is a dominant theme of those advocating self-determining rights in children today. Instead, Locke did not see the possibility of conflicting rights and advanced the argument that the child's good is the same as the parent's. Thus, parental benevolence is sufficient to insure the fulfillment of children's rights, whatever they are in Locke's view. In both Hobbes' and Locke's views there is a clear demand that parents control the lives of children according to preconceived notions of the children's future welfare. While Locke seems to want to constrain parental dominance of the child to some degree, well-meaning benevolence can be employed to manage the affairs of children with the same effect as explicit force. Both Hobbes and Locke posit the continued dependency of children on their parents without the right to make claims of their own.

John Stuart Mill does not perform any better than Hobbes or Locke in spite of his articulate defense of freedom and self-autonomy. The libertarian persuasion usually associated with Mill does not extend to his thinking about children. In fact, Mill assigns to the parents the mastery of the child. For Mill, "the existing generation is master both of the training and the entire circumstances of the generation to come."[12]

In granting the power of society over children to be absolute, Mill seems to disregard his principle of individual liberty which states: "An individual cannot rightfully be compelled to do or forbear because it will be better for him to do so, because it will make him happier, because in the opinion of others to do so would be wise or even right."[13]

Mill's proclaimed opposition to paternalism does not extend to children. "We are not speaking of children, or of young persons below the age which the law may fix as that of manhood or womanhood."[14]

While there is a need to protect children against the possibility of injury, it was Mill's thesis that freedom to make claims had no place unless a child was capable of rational discussion with resulting self-improvement. It was from a strictly utilitarian standpoint that Mill offered his strongest argument against allowing individual rights of self-autonomy to children.

With the need to maximize overall goodness in society, Mill feared that children would not act in accordance with the public good and therefore should not be permitted the right to interpret their own good. Thus, the exception to his arguments against paternalism was acceptable in the case of children because they are incapable of ascertaining what is in their own and society's best interest.

The law as it concerns the rights, privileges, obligations and protections of minors, presents a complex and continually evolving picture. For the most part, legal developments affecting minors have taken two directions. The first, commencing approximately 150 years ago, was the development of protective statutes and codes. The second, hardly 10 years old, emerges from recent court decisions affirming specific constitutional rights for minors. This second trend or direction will be dealt with more fully in the following chapters which take up specific rights of children.

As previously stated, children have received few rights under a system in which adults, institutions, and courts believed and assumed that they should act on behalf of the minor in his best interest. Such paternalistic acts, though for the most part benevolent, gave the young person virtually no voice at all. Only recently has there been any recognition that minors have substantial capacity to participate constructively in decisions affecting their lives long before they reach the age of 18.

The emerging protective statutes and codes which began in the nineteenth century were to be tailored to the needs of children rather than to a direct response to any rights they might possess. Needs were not necessarily rights. To say that a child needed to be protected from exploitation on the labor market was not to say that he had the legal or ethical right to be protected from such exploitation. The law does not recognize a need at its onset as a right. This is to say that a person cannot seek enforcement of a need by jural agencies. It is only when a need becomes coated with the element of enforcement that it becomes a legal right. By the same token, though it is argued as such by a few philosophers, a need is not an ethical right. To have a need for something does not necessarily establish a moral claim to it. Rooted within the statutes, codes, and court decisions was the continuing pretense that issues involving children are somehow above or beyond politics and that the parent-child relationship is private along with the family whose interests subsume those of children. Along with this is the belief that any failure to do what is best by a child is the exception, not the rule.

The legislation relating to children did not challenge the idea so firmly held in common law that children were the possession of parents. None of it expressed even a hint of granting status to the child as a person. This was to come some 170 years after the adoption of the Constitution of the United States. The movement began where it was most needed, in criminal jurisprudence, with the establishment of the first juvenile court in the

11

United States and in the world. This was in 1899 in Cook County, Illinois. From this beginning the concept spread throughout the nation and to other countries. Under the philosophy of the juvenile court system the young offender is not to be punished or stigmatized as he would be under adult criminal proceedings. He is to be helped in informal, closed, confidential hearings. The problem was, however, that children were also not to be accorded constitutional rights which are routinely accorded adults; and, in the absence of these rights, little attention was paid to the rights of due process of law.

Not until about 1890 did employment of very young children become virtually nonexistent; however, older children continued to be exploited until the 1930's. In many cases the minor had no choice in deciding where and whether or not to work. He or she was put to work by his or her parents to whom the wages were paid. Regulatory federal statutes restricting the employment of minors between 10 and 16 years of age were enacted three times but each time were struck down as unconstitutional. As a result, in 1920 only a fourth of minors between the ages 15 and 18 were in high school and approximately 12.5 million children aged 10 through 15 were employed. Many of these were employed in steel mills, mines and quarries.[15]

Only with the enactment of the Fair Labor Standards Act of 1938 did the exploitation of young minors begin to wane. This act prohibited the interstate shipment of goods to places of business that failed to follow the federal guidelines governing the employment of youths.[16] As a result of the Fair Labor Act, most states took the initiative and began to introduce complementary legislation prohibiting the employment of minors under 18 in hazardous industries and limiting the number of hours of work.

Through the ideal that acknowledges the right of children to an education, the concepts of children as persons and children's rights found their beginning. Initially, compulsory education laws were enacted simultaneously with labor laws to prevent a child from being sent to work instead of to school. In the 1930's nearly every state increased the minimum age for permissible ending of schooling from 14 to 16 years of age. This is generally the law today. The thrust of these reform laws has been to persuade society to treat children better. They provided a high degree of protection for minors as "privileged" members of society. However, they did not change the position of children within society or make them capable of securing better treatment for themselves. In reality, some of the protective directions of the statutes failed to safeguard the rights of certain minors as individuals and often resulted in serious inequities. Under the juvenile court system, a young offender may be deprived of his freedom for acts of disobedience which would not even be an offense if committed by someone over 18, (e.g., sexual promiscuity can result in juvenile court commitment although the same acts would not bring criminal penalties to an adult).

12

A petty theft by an adult may bring only a few months in prison while a similar offense by a 12-year-old minor may result in his confinement in a correctional institute for a period up to six years (i.e., until he has attained his adulthood).

While the reform laws responded to the demonstrations of children's needs, the first glimmering of the idea that children had any constitutional rights similar to adults began to emerge from some exemplary Supreme Court decisions. Prior to these decisions and after the enactment of the state school laws, the Supreme Court took care to reinforce and strengthen the parental right of supervision over children's education. However, these cases did not consider or deal with the rights of children as rights, but rather with the doctrine of parental right. They gave no consideration to the possibility that a parent may not be loyal to the interests of his or her child. In 1954, the Court moved to establish one of the first specific children's rights precedents in the case of *Brown v. Board of Education*.[17] It is not a landmark case for recognizing children as having rights of their own, such as is the later *Gault* case, but it took into consideration the constitutional rights of black school children.

In the Brown case, the Court held that the constitutional rights of black school children were violated through segregation in the public schools. The recognition of a right was narrow, but it was there.

> Today education is perhaps the most important function of state and local government . . . it is a principal instrument in awakening the child to cultural values, in preparing him for later professional training . . . in these days it is doubtful that any child may reasonably be expected to succeed in life if he is denied the opportunity of an education. Such an opportunity, where the state has undertaken to provide it, is a *right* which must be made available to all children.[18]

The Court's consideration for rights in education and its willingness to enforce those rights mark the *Brown* case as a significant precedent in this area.

Nowhere has the deprivation of rights been more evident than in juvenile courts. As I have previously stated, the laws governing juveniles charged with violations of the law have assumed the benevolence of state action. Prior to 1960 there was little law acknowledging that the Constitution required recognition of a child's right to certain procedural guarantees. It is not surprising then that the evolution of legal rights for minors began to take place in this area with an accompanying recognition of children as individual human beings having rights of their own. In 1967 the Supreme Court handed down its landmark opinion in *In re Gault* — the most famous children's rights case. This case holds a broad promise for children.[19]

13

In 1964 a young 15-year-old boy named Gerald Gault was arrested for making lewd phone calls. Subsequently he was adjudged a delinquent and sent to the Arizona State Industrial School for up to 6 years. Procedural rights, which are routinely afforded adults under the Bill of Rights, were violated, namely, timely notice of the charges (no notice of the charges was given until the day of the preliminary hearing), notification of the right to counsel (appointed by the court if necessary), the right to confront and cross-examine witnesses, and adequate warning of the privilege against self-incrimination with the right to remain silent. The Supreme Court ruled that the above basic guarantees of the Bill of Rights to due process must be provided for in juvenile court proceedings. We will see the importance of this ruling, particularly with respect to the notification of the right to counsel, in the more detailed discussion of the rights of children in mental institutions in Chapter 5.

The strength of the *Gault* case lies in its articulation that the Constitution is for minors also. In the majority decision, Justic Fortas stated: "Neither the Fourteenth Amendment nor the Bill of Rights is for adults alone."[20] Following its move in the *Gault case,* the Supreme Court finally put an end to the centuries old status of children as non-entities, by ruling in the case of *Tinker v. Des Moines School District* that children are "persons" under the Constitution.[21] In extending personhood to children, the court also removed some of the age old common law disabilities traditionally imposed upon children born out of wedlock,[22] and extended the protection of the First Amendment to the rights of students in public schools.[23]

If the Court had continued to pursue the broad promise of the *Gault* case, perhaps many of the bioethical dilemmas arising out of the treatment of children would not arise. However, since the *Gault* case the Court's decisions in some areas of children's rights have produced mixed and at times incongruous results. These decisions will be dealt with in discussing the position of the law today in the following Chapters.

The history of children's rights shows how children became persons. The laws discussed largely represent a set of rules and regulations ostensibly designed for the protection of children but often involving the restriction of their rights and the limitation of their ability to speak and act for themselves. Historically there has never been a "physician-patient" relationship where the "child" was the patient. It was always a "physician-parent" relationship. If we were to speak of rights of hospitalized children, we would speak of the rights of the parents of hospitalized children. The rights to privacy, of informed consent, or simply whether or not to seek medical treatment, were still over the horizon for children.

Before proceeding into the next chapter, it is necessary to touch on two important legal theories: the *Parens Patriae Power,* and the common law act of battery. Both of these theories play a critical role in any interpretation of children's rights regardless of the context in which they are asserted.

Under English law at the time of the American colonies, the King had the authority to act as the general guardian of all infants, idiots, and lunatics.[24] Prior to being vested in the King, the privilege and responsibility of caring for such persons belonged to the lord of the fee.[25] As sovereign, the King was responsible for the care and custody of all persons who were not possessed of their intellects or had become incompetent to take care of themselves.[26] The King, as parens patriae, was required to promote the interests and welfare of his wards and was not empowered to sacrifice the ward's welfare to the welfare of others.[27]

After the American Revolution, the parens patriae power became vested in the legislatures of the new states. These legislatures then began to delegate the authority to protect minors and incompetents to the courts. In the case of Mormon Church v. United States, the Court suggested that the parens patriae power is rooted in the very nature of the state.[28] It is inherent in the supreme power of every state and "often necessary to be exercised in the interest of humanity."[29] The doctrine of parens patriae can be seen as a power which society has granted the state for the protection of its future well-being.

The doctrine of parens patriae has been employed as the basis for state laws that allow for the involuntary commitment of the mental patient and which protect the interests of minors. In the 1845 decision of the Massachusetts Supreme Court, In re Oakes,[30] the Court said:

> The great law of humanity justified depriving an insane person of his liberty when his own safety or that of others required that he should be restrained for a certain time, and when restraint was necessary for his restoration, or would be conducive thereto.[31]

Historically then the parens patriae power was premised on the presumed incapacity of minors and the actual incapacity of idiots and lunatics to protect or care for themselves.[32]

The unconsented touching of one person by another constitutes, at common law, a battery for which damages may be recovered. The vital requirement is that the touching be unconsented.[33] The problem of all who are classified by law as "infants" is that they are viewed as incapable of giving effective consent to medical treatment or for that matter, consent to anything else. For this reason, physicians and hospitals facing liability for an unauthorized touching, have over the years often been unwilling to provide minors necessary treatment. Because touching is the essence of battery, it has long been held that a child is incapable of consenting to battery.[34]

From an historical perspective, even though an "infant" or "minor" gives consent to emergency treatment or treatment necessary to save his life, under the common law rule there would be a technical battery for

15

treating the child. His consent would not count. This can best be demonstrated by the case of *Rogers v. Sells*. In this case, the doctor amputated the foot of a 15-year-old boy where his right leg had been crushed so severely that all of the muscles, blood vessels, and nerves were torn and severed. There was no circulation in the leg. The doctor was held liable for battery in the absence of consent.[35]

With the two doctrines of *parens patriae* power and common law battery in hand, and the historical position of parental control, we can now move cautiously into the twentieth century and the emerging concepts of children's rights in treatment for mental and catastrophic illnesses.

CHAPTER 3

CATASTROPHIC ILLNESSES –
LEGAL RIGHTS

The whole family of biolegal and bioethical rights may be subsumed under the one broad right of self-autonomy – the right of a person to decide to do or not to do something. Thus there are the rights: to consent to treatment; to privacy; to participate in the decision-making process; to terminate treatment; to confidentiality in patient-physician relationship; to be truthfully informed; to have counsel; and many more. The enforcement of these rights and others not enumerated will vary according to the chronological, psychological, and physiological state of the person possessing them. For instance, it will be found that the assertion of a week old baby's right to consent to treatment is pragmatically different from that of a rationally competent adolescent, and we might conclude (erroneously or rightfully) that the right to express a "right" is more likely to be recognized and accepted by society the older a minor gets. We will also see that the law in most cases is more likely to give priority to the individual's chronological state in enforcing the right of autonomy, while ethical arguments which follow in Chapter 4 will tend to include and dismiss at times all three states – the chronological, psychological, and physiological.

The structure then of this chapter will be to analyze and discuss the law as it is applied by the courts in interpreting and enforcing statutes, codes, and existing case law dealing with children's rights. This chapter will be followed by a discussion in Chapter 4 of the ethical rights of children in treatment for catastrophic illnesses as they exist both together with and apart from the law. Chapter 4 will offer a general ethical framework within which one can ascertain those ethical rights that lend moral support to existing biolegal rights, as well as those rights that differ from the law and have no means for legal enforcement.

Generally, the law can be viewed as a complex interplay between two major sorts of factors: existing statutes and their various interpretations under case law, either in terms of what a court believes to be the legislative intent and meaning in a given set of circumstances or in terms of the statute's constitutionality; and, common and customary practice which may well be looked at to infuse meaning into archaic and often vague legal restrictions.

In the end whether a given action is legal or not, and whether certain rights are enforceable is, in each instance, a matter for the courts to determine on the basis of all the relevant factors.

In dealing with children's rights today, the law is not centered on any one position, instead, the law reinforces on the one hand the doctrine of strict parental control and decision-making, while on the other, it allows for some expressions of self-autonomy by children. For the most part, the law systematically continues to adhere to the idea of a chronological development or evolution of rights in children, although some notable exceptions have begun to appear which can provide the foundation for a new direction.

This chronological development of biolegal rights can be compared to existing law on assigning criminal and civil responsibility in children. In most jurisdictions, there can be no criminal or civil responsibility for a child under 7 years of age. There is a rebuttable presumption of such responsibility for minors between the ages of 7 and 14 years; and for minors over 14 years, full criminal responsibility exists.

The law does permit an accelerated acceptance of civil responsibility by the minor under the general doctrine of the "emancipated and mature" minor. The status of full emancipation can be bestowed by judicial decree on a minor 16-18 years of age thought to possess mature capacities; however, it is unlikley that a youth whose parents do not concur in his separation will be able to convince a judge that he or she should be formally emancipated. The minor is often at a further disadvantage in that he cannot pursue his own case in the courts. Generally, if parents are reluctant to concur in his liberation, or if the court deems him insufficiently mature, the emancipation decree will be withheld even though the minor's capacities may be to the contrary.[1]

There are specific instances where a minor may be partially emancipated for some purposes but not in general (e.g., to execute a contract or bill of sale to an automobile). This type of emanicipation extends only to the particular act to be performed and no further. Some statutes grant partial emancipation such as consent to sexual intercourse, or obtaining a driver's license.

The concept of "mature minor" is extremely limited in its application. It is used in juvenile court matters where a 16-year-old has committed a felony and the judge must decide whether or not to try the minor as an adult. It is also used to some extent now in cases involving 17-year-olds requesting emergency medical treatment. Here it has served often as a legal defense to parental charges of battery for treatment without consent. The central problem with the doctrine is the extraordinary inconsistency in what constitutes emancipation at different times in different states in statutory enactments. What counts as emancipation and maturity in one state can be discarded in the next state. What the law is and what possible new directions are opening up will now be discussed as we proceed to look at specific biolegal rights.

I. THE RIGHT TO CONSENT TO TREATMENT AND TO TERMINATE TREATMENT

Nowhere has there been a more positive movement toward according minors adult rights than in the matter of consent to medical care. In part this movement has arisen out of a recognition that many minors do have the capacity to make a valid informed consent. The recognition resembles the common law exception for emancipated minors and the emerging doctrine of the mature minor. [2] The extent and dimension of the minor's right to consent to treatment has not been completely determined by the courts, though some statutes seem to be clear in their import. Nevertheless, there is definitely a clear perceptible movement underway for granting some children some voice in the treatment they are to receive.

Prior to the emergence of any concept of children's rights in the matter of consent to medical treatment, the situation was largely governed by common law decisions relating to civil wrongs from unauthorized touching of a human being. It was also governed by the fact that a minor was ineligible to enter into a contract for medical care in the physician-patient relationship. The law assumed that only a parent could effectively consent to this relationship for his child. [3]

Thus, under common law rule it is a technical battery to treat a child without consent. Some jurisdictions have provided for judicial exceptions to the doctrine of battery by justifying a physician's conduct in these areas:

(1) Emergency treatment where the child's life is threatened.

(2) A wider range of treatments where a child is legally emancipated from his parents.

(3) Nearly any treatment where a child is close to the age of majority and it is reasonable to assume that under the circumstances his parents would not object.

Without question these judicial exceptions can favor a minor, or at least can prove to be beneficial to him, but they are, for the most part, exceptions to the law that work to relieve a physician from potential liability for treating the child. In the end they remain only that — judicial exceptions — and do nothing to foster the concept of the right to consent as a right.

Since a catastrophic illness goes far beyond the ordinary concept of every day medical needs (including birth control needs in the form of prescriptive contraceptives or pills, and abortions), it is difficult to comprehend the existence of any legal rights being vested in a minor which permit him to consent to a particular course of treatment for a catastrophic illness. For example, one may find it hard to conceive of permitting a 14-year-old child who is suffering from cancer of the colon to make the final decision on accepting or rejecting a colostomy, or, to refuse a life-sustaining blood transfusion because of religious convictions.[4] As explicated in Chapter 2, this difficulty can be traced to the reallocation of intergenerational roles and responsibilities, and to the state compelled extension of childhood. There is a social precept that children are to be shielded, wherever possible, from adult roles and responsibilties.

The question then becomes, in what circumstances should the law give children the power to decide such things for themselves and to be responsible for their own actions? In answering this question and in concerning oneself directly with the right to consent, one must deal with the broader question: How should power and responsibility be distributed among the relevant triad: the child, the family, and the state?

An evolution of the rights of minors in medical matters is beginning to take place in two areas of the law which deal with one specific issue: the right to consent to treatment. (1) Through the development of comprehensive legislative programs designed to cover all medical treatment of minors; and perhaps more importantly, (2) through a continuous series of judicial decisions directed toward establishing a constitutional basis for the right to consent to medical care within the right to privacy. The second area is considered the most important development because of the potentiality of adding constitutional dimension of the right to privacy to all facets of children's treatment for catastrophic illnesses. While legislative modifications are important, their ultimate success in the area of children's rights depends in the final analysis on judicial interpretations as to the intended scope of their application and constitutionality. Nonetheless, the most dramatic changes in the traditional rules of a child's right to consent to treatment lies in the development of comprehensive legislative programs and bears looking at carefully.

Legislation

As of 1977, 16 states have enacted and developed comprehensive statutes which relate to giving certain minors the authority to consent to medical treatment for certain specific conditions. With the possible exception of the states of Alabama and Louisiana, these statutes are narrowly constructed in their scope and apply for the most part to sensitive health problems of minors (e.g., adolescent sexual beahvior and drug abuse) and emergency care where there is a risk to "life or health." They do not meet the intended thesis of this essay — that of catastrophic illness.

Alabama's and Louisiana's liberal statutes may provide a different story. Under the Alabama statute, any minor who is 14 years or older, or has graduated from high school, or has been married, or is pregnant, or has borne a child may consent to any legally authorized medical treatment.[5] In addition no parental consent is required when in the physician's judgment, an attempt to secure consent would result in a delay of treatment which would increase the risk to the minor's life, health, or mental health.[6] While there has been no court interpretation of this section, it is reasonable to assume that an amputation of a mangled limb because of some catastrophic accident could be performed with only the minor's consent. Beyond that, however, it seems fairly clear that the legislative intent was to restrict the minor's right to consent to the specific areas set forth above. The Alabama statutes also allow a minor, regardless of age, to give effective consent to treatment of pregnancy, veneral diseases, drug dependency, or any reportable disease.[7]

The most liberal of all of the so-called new consenting statutes is Louisiana's.[8] This statute enacted in 1975, provides that *any* minor of *any* age who is or believes himself to be afflicted with any disease or illness may effectively consent to medical care and such consent will be valid. Even though this particular statute seems to be clear in its original intent — to provide to minors some degree of control over their ability to obtain medical treatment — it is unlikely that the legislative intent was to provide complete control over all areas of medical treatment to be received. For example, there is not the slightest hint that the law will permit a minor to refuse a prescribed course of treatment or to terminate treatment necessary to his general well being (i.e., blood transfusions or chemotherapy). Instead, the intent of these types of statutes appears to be more protectively oriented, both to the physician and to the patient, rather than to a clear legislative recognition of a right to self-determination. By permitting a minor to consent to treatment, the necessary condition for common law battery is removed. The physician and/or hospital is at once protected from any civil damages which might be pursued by parents of the consenting minor. These statutes respond to the pragmatic needs of general health care within society rather than to any recognized absence of minor's rights.

Without a clear recognition of the minor's right to control all matters of his medical treatment, it is doubtful that these statutes will have any effect beyond an initial consent to treatment when a minor patient is first hospitalized. The legislative modifications do serve a purpose however. The physician is forewarned as to what conduct will be protected. If, however, the care to which a minor may consent is limited, the effectiveness of his right to consent will be extremely qualified. Furthermore, the right to consent is denied to an entire class of capable children by establishing a minimum age below which the minor's consent is impossible. Only the state of Louisiana offers an exception to the minimum age rule. For the minor, the legislative exceptions, though beneficial, represent a piecemeal approach to a problem that is becoming increasingly serious.

Judicial Decisions

It is well established that an adult possesses a right under the common law to consent to medical care. This right is the foundation of the doctrine of informed consent which I will touch on in greater detail later. The right to refuse to submit to touching carries with it a right to knowingly accede to that touching.[9] Only recently have the courts begun to give constitutional dimensions to the right to consent and in so doing to provide for the preservation of self-autonomy. The constitutional dimensions are in evaluating the impact and propriety of consent as a privacy right. Through a fairly consistent series of cases interpreting and expanding the right to privacy, a substantital amount of case law is developing which can provide the basis for broader recognition of a minor's right to consent as a "right" per se. It is through this growing adult right to privacy and self autonomy that the evolving embryonic right to privacy for minors can be seen.

The adult.

In the study of the following line of cases, we will see that two concerns appear to underlie the right of privacy as articulated in these cases — protection of enumerated rights and preservation of self-autonomy. It is under the second concern — preservation of self-autonomy — that a minor's right to consent to treatment draws its greatest strength and is compatible with the ethical rights of minors that I will offer and argue for later on. With the adult right to privacy being firmly established, we can then understand the natural extension of the right to minors, with the conclusion that is the right does exist, it exists for the minor as well as the adult.

In the case of *Griswold v. Connecticut,*[10] the Supreme Court stated, "The recognition of a 'zone of privacy' serves to give a fuller meaning to several fundamental constitutional guarantees."[11] These words embrace the thesis that a person's particular interest may be declared to be a basic right though it is not specifically set forth in the constitution. The rationale which had its inception in this case and was to be expanded and clarified in the cases of *Roe v. Wade* and *Eisenstadt v. Baird*[12] which followed, is to the effect that the individual must maintain the ability to exercise his enumerated constitutional rights and that this included the ability to make a decision concerning a personal interest; that without this ability he might effectively lose them.

A clearer focus of this rationale can be seen by looking at the court's dictum in *Eisenstadt v. Baird.*[13] in extending the constitutional right of privacy to cover the matter of an individual's free consent to the use of birth control methods, the court said:

> If the right of privacy means anything, it is the right of the individual, married or single, to be free from unwarranted governmental interest into matters so fundamentally affecting a person as the decision whether to bear or begat a child.[14]

Continuing with its rationale, the court provided an even greater thrust to the evolving concept of personal autonomy within the right of privacy in the case of *Roe v. Wade.*[15]

What is so important in the *Roe* case and the thesis being developed here is the specific reference by the court to physical, psychological, and emotional harms that might interfere with an individual's ability to exercise his constitutional rights. If an interest is such that to deny it would produce physical, psychological or emotional harms that would effectively stand in the way of exercising any freedom guaranteed by the constitution that interest is protected by the constitution also.

The harms identified in the *Roe* case — physical, psychological and emotional — are not inherently limited to the abortion context. There is little room for debate that the individual's interest in his ability to seek, accept and consent to medical treatment other than abortion is also essential to his general well being. Thus, it would seem, that the *Roe* rationale, which mandates protection against those harms which effectively negate the individual's ability to exercise his enumerated freedoms under the consitution, applies with equal force to the individual's interest in his ability to consent to medical treatment.

In my discussion thus far, I have been talking about a competent adult's right to consent to treatment as guaranteed by the constitutional right of privacy. The existence of this basic adult right is a necessary condition if there is to be a recognition of any similar right in a minor. Because the protection of the constitution has been extended by the Supreme Court to include minors (in the *Gault* case discussed above), the discussed line of adult cases form the proper legal foundation, both in precedent and theory, for the onset of judicial decisions recognizing a minor's right to consent to treatment.

The minor.

As I pointed out at the conclusion of the previous chapter, the protections, afforded under the fourteenth amendment apply to any "person," and a minor is a person under the Constitution. The strongest

23

language positing this principle is contained in the *Gault* case where the court said, "Neither the Fourteenth Amendment nor the Bill of Rights is for adults alone."[16]

The two major cases delineating the minor's rights under the Constitution which strongly suggest that a minor has the same constitutional rights as an adult to consent to medical care are *In re Gault*[17] and *McKeiver v. Pennsylvania*.[18] We need to examine these two cases carefully to understand their relation to the question at hand — privacy to consent. We will then see the extension of the court's rationale in two important decisions that followed *Gault* and *McKeiver*.

The primary principle of *In re Gault* is, as mentioned, that the minor does possess rights under the constitution. In examining the question of rights, the court pointed out the traditional distinction between some rights that had been denied the minor because of the essential difference between adult and juvenile offenses — specifically, the right to a public trial and rights to bail. The minor was only subject to being "treated" and "rehabilitated" under a civil procedure, whereas the adult was formally accused of a crime, tried publicly, and if convicted, liable to punishment. It was felt that the criminal procedural rules applicable to adults were unnecessary for the minors. In looking at the denial of the procedural due process rights, the court said, "the condition of being a boy does not justify a Kangaroo Court."[19]

The court ruled that a minor is possessed of constitutional rights and accordingly, has a right to adequate notice of the charges against him, to counsel, to confrontation and cross-examination of witnesses, and to the sacred privilege against self-incrimination.

In the *McKeiver* case, the court considered the questions of a minor's right to a jury trial. The court, in distinguishing a juvenile detention hearing from a criminal trial, determined that a jury was not vital to the adjudicative stage of the juvenile justice system. Because the minor could obtain a fair trial from a judge as a fact finder, the court felt that there was adequate assurance that the child's rights will be protected.[20] It is important to point out that the court did *not* rule that the right to a jury trial did not exist if the minor were tried as an adult in a criminal court.

If we consider both the *Gault* case and the *McKeiver* case together, there is a clear indication that the minor does possess rights comparable to the adult under the Constitution. To abridge these rights, there must be a suitable substitute for the denied right, and this substituted alternative must maintain the benefit of the right for the child. This principle is very important in relating these cases to medical matters. We can accept the fact that there is no substitute for necessary medical care. It is not sufficient to qualify the commitment of such care on the presence of a parent. For example, a minor whose parents cannot or will not consent to a particular course of medical treatment for a catastrophic illness, may be denied the right to be heard. Applying this example to the juvenile offender, we can see that the minor can at least be heard at a hearing, where he might not be heard at all in a hospital. The rule that parental consent is required even for minors able to evaluate their own condition and the treatment available to them, can be a severe liability. (I will discuss this last proposition at some depth in the sections on ethics.)

Since establishing the rationale of the *Gault* and *McKeiver* cases, the Supreme Court in two important cases has extended the constitutional dimensions of the right to privacy in minors. In looking at these cases, two important aspects are noted: (1) Both cases are directly related to the issue of consent in medical matters and provide a possible connecting link to the right of a minor having total control over his own body. And, (2) the court fails to establish a criteria for balancing the compelling interest of the state with the consitutional rights of minors. It is the absence, at this time, of any clear understanding of the scope of the compelling interest of the state that ultimately forestalls a final disposition to the issue of a minor's right to control what will be done to his body while he is in treatment for a catastrophic illness. From these cases, there is room, however, to maintain the position that, at least from age 14 up, the minor's point of view should be sought before a decision is made.

As in the *Roe v. Wade* case,[21] the court selected the controversial question of abortion to enlarge the concept of the right to privacy. In the case of *Planned Parenthood of Central Mo. v. Danforth*,[22] the court ruled that medical procedure to terminate pregnancy can be undertaken by an unmarried minor without the express consent of her parents. The court stated that a state cannot require the consent of the parent or person *in loco parentis* as a condition of abortion of an unmarried minor during the first 12 weeks of her pregnancy.[23] In its application of the minor's right to privacy the court felt in cases of abortion, "the state does not have the constitutional authority to give a third party an absolute and possibly arbitrary veto."[24]

For the first time the Supreme Court recognized the right of a minor to act autonomously within the constitutional right of privacy in making a serious medical decision. The groundwork for this decision was laid in the *Roe v. Wade* case[25] and in the isolated state case of *State v. Koome*.[26] The *Roe* case, of course, invoked adult standards. However, the *Koome* case dealt specifically with a minor and involved a direct confrontation with parental authority in a medical context. A physician was convicted of performing an abortion on a 16-year-old, unmarried, pregnant girl in contravention of a statute prohibiting anyone from aborting any woman under 18 without the consent of her parent or guardian. The girl had petitioned the court for an order granting her the abortion. Her petition was opposed by her guardian, the Catholic Children's Society, and her parents. The lower court granted her petition. However, her parents appealed to the Washington Supreme

25

Court for a stay of the abortion pending the final outcome of the litigation. Meanwhile, the doctor proceeded to perform the abortion and was subsequently prosecuted for his actions as violating the prohibitive criminal statute. The doctor challenged the statute on the grounds that it violated the right of an unmarried minor to terminate her pregnancy without unreasonable governmental restraint as well as the equal protection clause. The court overturned the statute on both grounds holding that *prima facie,* the constitutional rights of minors, including the right of privacy, are coextensive with those of adults.

While the *Koome* case was originally initiated from the legal imposition of certain religious mores, the final participating parties were the same, and the compelling interest of the state versus the minor's right to privacy was the ultimate issue to be determined by the court. Since the *Planned Parenthood* decision,[27] the court's decisions have been fairly congruous in holding that a minor's right to privacy in determining to have an abortion is the superior right.

It is the case of *Carey v. Populations International Services, Inc.,*[28] decided by the Supreme Court in June 1977, that leaves us somewhat perplexed and confused as to how far the court is prepared to go with the rights of minors in a medical setting. *Carey* is a powerful case and the dictum on minor's rights is far-reaching. However, the court's articulation is admittedly hesitant in providing us with any definitive limits on the autonomous activity of a minor.

In the case, the lower District Court held unconstitutional a New York statute which made it unlawful for non-prescriptive contraceptives to be distributed to any minor under 16 years of age except by licensed physicians. On appeal the appellant (the state) contended that the provision of the New York act is constitutionally permissible as a regulation of the *morality* of minors, in furtherence of a state's interest against promiscuous sexual intercourse among the young. Thus, a direct confrontation of the state's interest versus minor's right to privacy was before the court.

In the initial part of its decision, the court was quick to extend the rationale of *Roe v. Wade*[29] and the *Planned Parenthood* case[30] — that terminating a pregnancy was certainly more serious than the purchase and use of contraceptives.

Of particular significance to the decision of this case, the right to privacy in connection with decisions affecting procreation extends to minors as well as adults.

The court again affirmed *In re Gault,*[31] holding that "minors, as well as adults, are protected by the constitution and possess contitutional rights."[32] The court then cited *Planned Parenthood*[33] stating, "State restrictions inhibiting privacy rights of minors are valid only if they serve

26

any significant state interest that is not present in the case of any adult."[34]

It is the scope of the phrase "any significant state interest that is not present in the case of adult" that takes us nowhere and continues to haunt the court. The Supreme Court, obviously concerned with any misinterpretation as to the extent of the minor's right recognized in the case, is cognizant of its own hesitation to define the totality of the minor-state relationship.

> The question of the extent of state power to regulate conduct of minors not constitutionally regulatable when committed by adults is a vexing one, perhaps not susceptible to precise answer. We have been reluctant to attempt to define the totality of the relationship of the juvenile and the state.[35]

In viewing the problem, the court seems to leave the state control of the minor in certain matters, yet compels the state to justify any attempts to exercise this control when such control burdens the exercise of a fundamental right. It is a tightrope with apparently no end. There are no definitive criteria for determining priorities. Instead, each case is treated differently and must be examined individually for an isolated decision. This gives us a lot to unpack by way of interpreting the direction of the present drift of the Supreme Court in regards to children's rights. For example, the court said in *Ginsburg v. New York*:

> The principle is well settled that a state may permissibly determine that, at least in some precisely delineated areas, a child is not possessed of that full capacity for individual choice which is essential to the exercise of various constitutionally protected interests.[36]

And again in *Prince v. Massachusetts*, "Restraints on the freedom of minors may be justified 'even though' comparable restraints on adults would be constitutionally impermissible."[37]

The court does not attempt to tell us when a child is unable to make an individual choice. To do so, it seems, would call for an arbitrary decision. Instead, the burden of justifying restraints on the freedom of minors is placed on the state. The state must show somehow lack of "full capacity."

> When a state burdens the exercise of a fundamental right, its attempt to justify that burden as a rational means for the accomplishment of some significant state policy requires more than a *bare* assertion, based on a conceded complete absence of supporting evidence, that the burden is connected to such a policy.[39]

Thus, a state is prohibited from arbitrarily infringing upon a minor's fundamental right to privacy. The prohibition must be justified as a necessary condition to remove an alleged ominous threat to the continuing

27

health, life, or well-being of a minor. What remains unclear, however, is the "how to" in ascertaining when there has been a proper justification for a state policy. So often the policy in question is a direct result of the existing moral climate of the state, which when judicially interpreted or enforced, is not always necessarily compatible with certain fundamental guarantees of the Constitution. An example of this principle can be seen in the *Carey case*.[39]

In the *Carey* case, the State of New York argued that to permit the sale of contraceptives to minors under the age of 16 would work to undermine the state's interpretative moral policy of discouraging sexual promiscuity among children. The court felt, however, that the state failed to justify its assertions that its policy was essential to health, life and well-being of minors. Yet the court's own paranoia on the question is demonstrated by the previously cited *Ginsburg* case.[40] This case seems to be in direct conflict with the *Carey* case. In *Ginsburg,* the state of New York enforced its obscenity statute by prosecuting the defendant Ginsburg for the sale and distribution of alleged pornographic literature. The same moral policy was invoked — permitting minors access to pornography will lead to sexual promiscuity.

The Supreme Court held that in the area of pornography a child is not possessed of "that full capacity" for individual choice which is essential to the exercise of the constitutional right of privacy. Thus we see the legal antithesis that a 15-year-old child *is* possessed of "that full capacity" in determining to purchase contraceptives for sexual intercourse, but is *not* possessed of "that full capacity" in determining to purchase literature depicting acts of sexual intercourse. In both cases, the court reaffirmed the principle that the power of the state to control the conduct of children reaches beyond the scope of its authority over adults.

Where do these decisions leave us in regard to the issue of this inquiry — the minor's right to claim the right of privacy while *in* treatment for catastrophic illnesses? We know that children are, at least in some areas of the law, on comparable and equal footing with adults in the exercise of constitutional rights,[41] particularly the right to privacy. We also know that the power of the state to control the conduct of children reaches beyond the scope of its authority over adults. It is not, however, a power that can be arbitrarily exercised by the state, by any means. If the power is questioned or contested by a minor, the state must be prepared to demonstrate clearly and convincingly that the minor does not have the "full capacity" to understand and make an individual choice with reference to the particular interest being protected by the state. The problem here is that the interpretation of "full capacity" is generally an arbitrary one or is closely connected to the chronological development of a minor. Some states, for example, have established the age of sexual consent at 16, while others maintain "full capacity" to comprehend the nature of the act is attained as early as 14 years. Outside of the line of cases dealing with issues of abortion and birth control, there are only a handful of cases which can assist us in speculating on how far the right to privacy will carry a minor in controlling the decision-making process in catastrophic medical cases. While the medical procedure employed in aborting a fetus is certain a serious undertaking, it can hardly be classified as catastrophic in scope. (In any event, the minor's final right to consent to an abortion is given a narrow birth by the Supreme Court.)

It will help us now to turn to an actual case study of an adolescent in treatment for a diagnosed catastrophic illness.[42]

The medical records indicate the patient is a 15-year-old white male suffering from osteosarcoma of the left leg. The site of the bone lesion is in an area three inches below the knee. The course of treatment recommended to the patient's parents is amputation of the leg at a point five inches above the knee. After the amputation, there will be a six-week period of intensive chemotherapy.

The prognosis for a full recovery can be broken down into four categories: (1) No treatment, 100% terminal. (2) No amputation, but chemotherpy, 95% terminal. (3) Amputation, but no chemotherapy, 20% recovery. (4) Amputation and chemotherapy, 35-40% recovery. Thus, even with the most effective treatment available, (4) — the prognosis for full recover is not good. There is a side note, however; one that must be taken into consideration also in reaching a decision. There is a definite risk in the treatment itself. For example, in the case in question, with the employment of chemotherapy, there is a 5% risk of fatality. Therefore, patients selecting (4) — the most effective course of treatment — are faced with a 5% fatality risk from the treatment itself, while those opting for (3) do not face the added risk though the percentage of recovery is one-half that of (4). There are, of course, other factors that might be considered in the decision-making process: the risk of the operation, loss of bodily integrity, the disabling effect from chemotherapy, and many others.

Obviously, with the multiple variables present in the proposed treatment, a legal informed consent is necessary. But from whom? Does the unemancipated minor have the right to accept or reject any of the options (1), (2), (3), or (4), taking what we might reasonably suppose the law to be today? This is to say, that if the minor were put to the test in a court for the right to exercise the constitutional right to privacy, as in the abortion cases, would it be granted?

The standard of comparison for the ultimate right of the minor is, of course, the adult right — what is permissible and reserved to an adult. While an adult enjoys all of the constitutional rights enjoyed by a minor, the reverse is not true. The adult standard can be seen in the cases of *Roe v. Wade*[43] and *Griswold v. Connecticut*[44] which were cited as precedent for invoking the right to privacy in the case of *Planned Parenthood*.[45] The

29

minor's right to control procreation was compared to the adult's right to privacy in that type of matter. If we are to make some reasonable transition to the category of catastrophic illnesses, we need to understand better the standard being applied to adults. This standard can be derived from the principle of informed consent. Though I will discuss informed consent more thoroughly under a separate section to follow, it is necessary to take a brief look at the principle to tie in the adult standard.

Simply stated, the principle of informed consent holds that an adult patient must be given information on the risks involved in the treatment he is about to receive and he must consent to that treatment. The physician must impart to the patient adequate information on the type of treatment in order to permit the patient to make a rational and free assent to the treatment. The basis of this principle is the patient's right to privacy in determining what shall be done with his own body.[46]

In the leading case of *Canterbury v. Spence*,[47] the court noted that it is well established that a patient has a right to decide what shall be done with his own body, but that the patient can effectively exercise this right only if he has been properly informed by his doctor as to his condition. The adult right to retain control over decisions about treatment to be received includes both the right to consent to that treatment and the right to refuse treatment. However, it should be noted here that this is a general rule and that the court in *Canterbury v. Spence* is referring explicitly to the *competent* adult patient, where the issue of rationality is not in question. Obviously, if the patient were judged to be incompetent he would stand in no greater stead than a minor whose rationality had not been recognized and would be an exception to the general rule.[48] There are a few cases holding that a minor is entitled to informed consent along with his parents.[49] However, informed consent does not at this time carry the same full rights for the minor as it does for the adult. A minor might be entitled to informed consent, but in most cases this can be accomplished by informing the parent. Thus, from the case law cited involving adults, it seems clear that an adult, if fully informed, would have the *prima facie* right to accept or reject any of the options (1), (2), (3), and (4).

There are at this time only a handful of court decisions dealing with minors in contested medical matters. For the most part, the basic issue being contested is the conflict between a parental decision on the one hand and the state's invocation of the doctrine of *parens patriae* on the other. There is no case of record at this time, where the minor is the moving party to the litigation in attempting to enforce the right to exclusively decide his course of treatment. To understand the minor's dilemma in the decision-making process, it will help us to look at a few recent cases that hint at his right to decide.

In *In re Green*[50] a 16-year-old boy suffered from polio. His physician recommended a spinal fusion as a remedy for his condition. While polio is a catastrophic illness, in this particular case there was no evidence that the boy's condition endangered his life or that the medical procedure had to be performed immediately. To the contrary, the operation carried with it a risk factor in there being some level of danger to the boy's health. The mother, a Jehovah's Witness, agreed to the operation but would not permit a transfusion if needed during the operation. This fact made the performance of the operation impossible. The state as *parens patriae* sought a court order compelling the operation and transfusion. The critical issue of the operation or the child's life was not involved.

The Pennsylvania court viewed the case as a conflict between parental autonomy in decision making, which included the right to freely exercise religious beliefs and the state's interest in protecting the child. The court found that state's interest did not outweight parents' interest because the child's life was not threatened. The court, however, from its decision, appeared to decide the case on a broader basis than parental rights.[51] "The ultimate question is whether a parent's religious beliefs are paramount to the possible adverse decisions of the child."[52]

The court remanded the case to the lower court to determine the views of the child on the subject. On remand, the child testified that he did not want the operation, and the trial court refused to order the treatment. An implication can be drawn that the child's right to consent to treatment can and should be a significant factor in resolving a conflict of his interest and parent's interest in following religious practices.

The implication from *Green* is given support by an earlier New York case, *In re Seiferth*.[52] This case concerned a 12-year-old boy who suffered from a congonital harelip and cleft palate. The boy's defect gave him a hideous appearance and made him emotionally and psychologically sensitive to his condition. The state petitioned the children's court for an order authorizing an operation to cure his physical defects. The boy's father, while not voicing a religious objection to the operation, believed that forces in the universe would cure his son. The court did not immediately order the operation; instead, it ordered that the child speak with other individuals, without the interference of his father, about the benefits accruing to him from promptly submitting to the recommended operation. The decision of whether to submit to the operation or not was left to the child. When the child decided to wait for "the natural forces to cure him," the court refused to order the treatment. "It would appear," the court stated, "that the child's decision, even if it is misguided, does merit some consideration by the state."

The court's view in *Seiferth* was cited by Justice Douglas in his dissenting opinion in *Wisconsin v. Yoder*.[54] "Where the child is mature enough to express potentially conflicting desires, it would be an invasior of the child's rights to permit an imposition without canvassing h views."[55]

31

It should be noted in the *Seiferth* and *Green* cases that there was an obvious underlying influence on each child's decision by the parent's religious interest. The contest between parental religious interest, *parens patriae*, and the child's interest does not lend itself to a clear decision — one on which we can hang our hat. If the parent's religious beliefs are allowed to override the child's right to consent to medical care, that age of discretion may never be reached. When, to allow parents to exercise their rights would create a severe and immediate threat to the right of their child to health and life, those parental rights must give way to the rights of the child.

A number of courts have authorized medical care over parental objection, whether based on religious grounds or not, when the life of the child weighed in the balance. For example, in the case of *People ex re v. Labrenz*,[56] the court ordered a blood transfusion for a dying child over the objection of parents who were Jehovah's Witnesses. One court has gone as far as ordering an operation upon birth for an unborn child where parental denial of a blood transfusion at birth seemed likely.[57] It thus appears that when the action or inaction of the parent threatens the child's life, there is a justification under *parens patriae* to override the parental objections.

Some courts have failed to apply this rationale when the child's life was not at stake but only a serious health problem. In the case of *In re Hudson*,[59] the court would not order an operation to correct an arm deformity. This case closely follows the *Green* case.[59] A few courts have ordered nonvital care in such situations over parental and child objection. In *In re Sampson*[60] the court ordered a blood transfusion despite the religious objections of the boy's mother, even though the operation was not necessary. It appears the reason for the distinction in the cases and the court's rationale in intervening is that the state's interest is diminished by the absence of immediate peril to the life of a child from a failure to order an operation. It would seem, however, that the interests of both the child and the state may be just as strong in this situation.[61]

> If parents are not permitted to make martyrs of their children (by refusing blood transfusions), there is little argument for allowing them to make their children physical or psychological cripples by denying them needed care.

In any event, the injury to the child's right is different only in degree, and this difference in degree does not affect the constitutional status of the right to consent. Where the state has intervened even though the child's life was not at stake,[62] the court has based its decision on the state's paramount duty to insure the child's right to live and grow up without disfigurement.

It is time now to briefly pause and take stock of where we are with the legal issue of a minor's right to consent to medical treatment. In looking back we can see that minor's rights in medical matters have been affected by two areas of the law: (1) Statutory and (2) Case law. While the new consenting statutes appear *prima facie* to grant to the minor an unlimited right to consent to medical treatment, they have yet to be given a definitive interpretation as to how extensive this right to consent is. Whether or not their intent is to restrict the right to consent to emergency treatments, or go beyond to include any medical decision, must await a judicial interpretation. It is felt at this time that the statutes are applicable only to emergency type decisions, or ones related to treatment for veneral diseases and abortions. For example, even though the Louisiana statute[63] grants to minors of any age the right to consent to treatment, it is hardly imaginable, in the light of present case làw, that the legislature intended to permit a 7-year-old boy the right to consent to open heart surgery without parental permission.

The present state of case law is not quite so speculative. There appear to be three fairly clear delineated areas of rights. (1) If the medical matters are of such a personal and private nature, then the child's right is supreme unless the state can successfully carry the burden of proving a compelling interest to the contrary. (2) Consent for surgery and other medical treatment is a widely recognized parental prerogative. Even though the cases which most strongly support parental power in this area involve very young children, it is nevertheless thought to be the general rule that in determining the need for surgical or hospital treatment, the personal consent of the child need not be obtained. (3) In certain circumstances, the state may place judicial limitations upon freedom of minors and parental discretion. The majority of the authorities restrict the state's interest under *parens patriae* to those cases where the life of the minor is endangered. In concluding this section, we can say that while the body of case law on consent to surgery and other medical treatment for catastrophic illness does not explicitly recognize a new role for children, the limitation of parental power in the name of the state may have the practical effect of upholding the child's interest.

II. INFORMED CONSENT

In the preceding section, I briefly focused on the important principle of informed consent. My discussion of the principle was necessary to demonstrate and establish the adult standard as the ultimate in a patient's right to determine what shall be done with his own body. We need now to look more closely at this important principle in relation to children in treatment for catastrophic illnesses. In doing so we will see that there is a distinction between a "consent to treatment" and an "informed consent."

It would seem that if a minor does not have the right to consent to a particular course of treatment for a catastrophic illness, any discussion of

33

informed consent is ludicrous. The term "informed" is, however, a "legal" qualifying factor. It tells us what kind of consents are valid; that a legally effective consent must be informed. While a partially informed consent might relieve a physician of common law battery, it would be insufficient to protect him from liability for injuries resulting from an undisclosed risk. Legal-medico jurisprudence requires that a physician obtain the consent of a patient before performing surgery unless the need for such is obviated by an emergency which places the patient in immediate danger and makes it impractical to secure such consent. The authorities consider an "effective consent" one which is made after the patient has been advised of the possible consequences and risks inherent in the particular operation.[64]

Before a patient will be deemed to give an informed consent, it may be necessary that he know the alternative methods of treatment available to him and the inherent dangers and possiblities of success of such alternatives. The philosophy behind such a theory of informed consent is that the patient has the right and responsibility to determine whether he or she wants to risk the suggested surgery. He must understand in addition to the risks of the suggested surgery, the possible results of the failure to chance it. Thus, under this theory, a consent is informed only if the patient knows what is apt to happen to him or her and the possible adverse results and dangers of the operation. A minor's right to informed consent is in most cases disregarded under this theory because of presumed lack of capacity to understand.

There is another theory on informed consent which should be noted, one which has implications in children's rights.[65] As a qualifying factor to the action of consent, "informed" in its application to adults, does not mean that a patient must actually comprehend the matter he has been informed of, but only that he has been informed of the matter. There is the general assumption that an adult (unless known to the contrary) is competent and has the capacity to understand. The presumption of this "capacity" does not at present extend to minors. It is chronologically determined. (For example, at age 18, a minor automatically becomes an adult. The capacity to consent to sexual relations is arbitrarily set by the states.) Its presumed absence is the chief underlying factor in denying to minors, as a class, the right to consent to treatment, let alone be informed. Under this second theory, the legal argument presented is that although implying that the decisive factor is the patient's ability to understand, actually informed consent involves only a duty to disclose on the part of the physician; it is the opportunity to decide rather than the actual ability to understand.

This rationale is followed in the case of *Canterbury v. Spence*[66] where the court held that the physician was liable if he breached the duty to inform — not if the patient fails to understand. It would seem then, on the first level at least, that this rationale can be extended to children, if the primary principle is the opportunity to understand rather than the actual ability to understand.

This position is followed by the Department of Health, Education and Welfare insofar as issuing grants for experimentation on children. In HEW Guidelines for 1973, there is the requirement that children participate fully in the decision-making process for non-therapeutic experimentation.[67] They must be fully informed of the proposed protocol even though they might not have the actual ability to understand it. In these types of cases both the child's and his parents' consents are required. This requirement was also followed in the case of *Merriken v. Cressman*.[68] The court held that the informed consent of both the parent and the child was necessary as a constitutional prerequisite for procedures not affirmatively sought by the child, but instituted for reasons of public benefit. In this case proposed tests had been offered to an unconsenting teenager in an effort to identify potential drug abusers. The failure to obtain informed consent violated the constitutional right to privacy. A possible factor that might distinguish this case from others was the presence of criminal liability for drug abuse. There was the element of self-incrimination by the unconsenting minor in participating in a program in which he did not know how the results might be used.

Thus, in concluding, it is sufficient to say that the exceptions to the rule of informed consent are identical to those exceptions previously enumerated to the general requirement of parental consent. In those specific areas where a minor's consent is permitted (e.g., abortion) and is sufficient by itself, the medical personnel involved are legally required to obtain an effective informed consent. In the other cases, the "informed" factor is directed to and sought from the parent or legal guardian.

III. THE RIGHT TO COUNSEL

As far as the law is concerned, there is a clear distinction between a medical hosptial and a mental hospital. While someone might propose an ethical argument that there are certain similarities in patient-status, the law thus far has drawn no such comparison. The distinguishing factor is "commitment to" and threat of incarceration in mental hospital that ultimately provides the patient with the right to counsel. There is a due process right to counsel in every case where a patient is threatened with imprisonment. Because the admission to a medical hospital does not carry with it a legal interpretation or imprisonment, there is no case law or statutory law which recognizes a minor's right to counsel in such a setting. There is no procedure whereby a minor can be detained beyond his medical healing period unless mental health commitment statutes are invoked. In such a case, the minor then would have the constitutional guarantee of due process and the right to counsel.

Generally speaking, any minor-parent disagreement over accepting or rejecting a particular course of treatment is resolved through a parental decision. This is not to say, however, that the minor's interests go unprotected. While a minor's singular opposition to surgery or other medical procedure is an insufficient ground for court appointed counsel, the minor, if the opposition is serious enough, may be joined by the hospital, doctor, or state in opposing the parental decision. In a case of this type, a formal court proceeding would be necessary, and the minor is entitled to full representation before the court either by counsel of his choice, or through a court appointed counsel. We can safely conclude at this time, that a minor is not entitled to counsel as a matter of right, upon being admitted to a medical hospital for treatment of a catastrophic illness.

IV. RIGHT TO CONFIDENTIALITY

The question of confidential communications within a medical setting becomes extremely thorny when the patient is a minor. As we will see later, it is almost unsolvable in the setting of a mental hospital. While the solutions provided by the law seem to be adequate, at least from the pragmatic functioning of society, the ethical dilemmas are enormous. We are concerned at this time only with the position of the law.

All fifty states require that full medical records be maintained by hospitals and other health care institutions. In many cases, the hospital-licensing regulations establish the minimum requirements as to what information must be present in the medical record. Even though the medical record is the property of the hospital, the hospital is charged with the responsibility of protecting the confidentiality of the patient's record. In most states the record is protected by law from unauthorized inspection.[69] The law has also established that the personal data contained in the record are confidential because of the special relationship between patient and physician.

It is the status as a patient that thus gives the minor the right to confidentiality in communications in a medical setting. This right is *prima facie* at the most because it is qualified by the patient's status as a minor. The principle of confidentiality is based upon the special relationship established between the patient and his physician or hospital. This relationship is both a fiduciary relationship and a contractual relationship. While a minor can enjoy a fiduciary relationship, he does not establish a contractual relationship with his doctor or with the hospital. This fact, along with the fact that the parent is the legally contracting party for medical services to the minor, permits the legal intrusion of the parent in the minor's right of confidentiality. Thus, unless excluded specifically by statute, the minor's right to confidentiality is included within his or her parent's right to confidentiality.

Whenever the record is to be used outside the confidential relationship, written authorization is required of the parent. Insofar as the parent-child relationship, this is a unilateral prerequisite, in that only the parent's signature is necessary. A minor has the right to confidentiality in his medical records only so far as his parents desire to keep the records confidential.

An exception to the above law is provided by those states which have authorized the minor to consent to medical treatment.[70] For example, a minor who is receiving treatment for veneral disease is protected from any disclosure of his medical record. The record of a minor who has obtained an abortion without parental consent is protected.

The underlying principle here is that of the right to privacy. The nature of the treatment is of such an intimate nature that knowledge of the treatment can be detrimental to the general well being of the minor, and in the case of the parent, could become a disruptive force in the harmony of the family. This same rationale supports the thesis on confidentiality discussed in the chapters on catastrophic and mental illnesses.

Since we are concerned with catastrophic illnesses, these types of cases are really irrelevant. In every instance, where the minor is in treatment for a catastrophic illness, a parent, guardian or the state will be directly involved. And though the court has held that a patient's interest in keeping confidential communication from public purview was constitutionally protected, it was not meant to deny the parent, guardian, or the state status as a party to the confidentiality.

CHAPTER 4

CATASTROPHIC ILLNESSES – ETHICAL RIGHTS

I. "THE THEORY OF JUSTICE" – RAWLS AND DWORKIN

In the second chapter I briefly discussed three philosophers – Hobbes, Locke and Mill – all of whom wrote extensively on human rights, but with little concern for children's rights. In fact, any argument in favor of self-autonomous rights being vested in children would find little comfort from the three, especially Mill, who for all his dedication to the cause of individual liberty, explicitly denied self-determinative rights to the minor. In his view the position of the child in relation to his parent and the state was permanently fixed. Unlimited paternalism is acceptable in the case of children because they are incapable of deciding what is in their own and society's best interest.

Jeremy Bentham perhaps sums up the minor's position.

The feebleness of infancy demands protection. Everything must be done for an *imperfect* being, which as yet does nothing for itself. The complete development of its physical powers takes years; that of its intellectual faculties still slower. At a certain age, it has already strength and passions, without experience enough to regulate them. Too sensitive to prevent impulses, too negligent of the future, such a being must be kept under an authority more immediate than that of the laws.[1]

The term "authority more immediate" for Bentham meant "parental authority." Bentham's remarks underscore the socio-legal concept of the ineptness of children as a class to rationally express a claim.

Even the flaming liberals of today, such as Nozick, Berlin, and Feinberg, who are the fiercest opponents of paternalism, do not hesitate to accept it for children. They consistently manipulate the definition of man in such a way that one can embrace the doctrine of equal liberty for adults while maintaining paternalism for children. The chorus of agreements is to the effect that the idea of a firm boundary between the stages of childhood and adulthood should be maintained – that there are marked differences in the capacities of children and adults that justify a paternalistic society insofar as children are concerned. There is a major problem with their views, however, in that the morally relevant differences between the two stages cannot be reduced to a single factor such as age, ability to make rational decisions, or the ability to be self-sufficient.[2] No allowance is made for the possibility of a common value which transcends both stages and which will support at times both an anti-paternalistic view and a paternalistic view.

An interesting and adequate framework for children's rights, however, can be established in the context of John Rawls's theory of justice. As will be shown, to assert rights to fair treatment, as Rawls does, is to assert an obligation on the part of adults to acknowledge the just claim of children. This claim in Rawls's thesis is just and as such is consistent with the procedural principles of justice on which society should be established. These principles extend to children as well as adults.[3] We will see that the theory of justice provides the framework for a moral justification of the various legal rights enumerated and is the basis of the whole range of moral rights I will claim should be supported by society and judicially recognized.

To begin with, Rawls bases his theory of the just society on a particular kind of social contract. His system of justice requires that people "understand the need for, and they are prepared to affirm, a characteristic set of principles for assigning basic rights and duties and for determining what they take to be the proper distribution of the benefits and burdens of social cooperation."[4]

Within this view is a goal that will allow each person to act according to an individual conception of his own best interests, but not at the expense of others.

To attain the just society, individuals engage in mutual determination of evolving principles of fair treatment for everyone in the present and in the future. The central thesis is that everyone participates in selecting these principles, and that they are to be thought of as chosen in an "original position" where every individual is ignorant of his own specific circumstances and interests in real life. It is this ignorance of their position in real life that guarantees that the individual will select principles of

39

justice impartially, with equality in mind, thus assuring that no individual is compelled to serve as an instrument of the interests of others, or that, if he is compelled to serve all will do so equally.

Rawls allows for three constraints on selfishness in selecting the principles of justice: that individuals possess some understanding as to what might constitute an adequate theory of justice; that they be rational in choosing; and, that their choices be made behind a "veil of ignorance." Rawls then offers that, assuming the three constraints are met, only one set of principles of justice will emerge. All of the participants in society will see that it is in their interest to arrive at the same general conclusion about adequate rules for a system of justice. For Rawls there will be unanimity to the principles.

There are two fundamental principles of justice that everyone will agree upon: First, that each individual should have the most extensive personal liberty possible compatible with a like liberty for all others. This is to say that no person should have more liberty than anyone else to pursue his or her goals in life. Secondly, that individuals must share equally whatever advantages or disadvantages societal inequalities bring. This second principle is primarily intended to preclude discrimination against those born into a societal inequality such as poverty. These two fundamental principles establish the foundation for the entire system of justice as fairness and equal respect and concern.

Rawls argues that in the original position, because of self-interest, persons would want initially to assure their own individual freedoms and to do this would at the beginning make the assumption that other persons might want to restrict these freedoms. With this, then, the individual's initial intent would be to establish guarantees of his or her own liberty, to assure the preservation of personal liberty. Along with this minimal personal freedom, there is a like grant to everyone else and restricting conditions on one's own freedom as one would wish the freedom of others to be restricted.

Rawls further argues that in the construction of the system, any submission to restriction of society would be bilateral in that no person would opt to submit to restrictions without expecting a like submission from others. All those who submit to the restrictions would demand a just claim against all others in society. Therefore, *every person* would have a right to demand equal respect and concern from their fellows. The justification for this critical right is based on the fact that everyone has freely consented to make themselves subject to the claims of everyone else.

An important aspect of Rawls is that he provides some sort of framework for applying the principles of justice. Briefly, Rawls supposes that the parties to the original position will move to a constitutional convention after they have adopted principles of justice. At this point they are to select a constitution and decide upon the justice of political forms.

Out of this convention will come a system for the constitutional power of government and the basic rights of citizens. It is essential here that the ignorance about particular individual traits continue, as well as about one's social positions, concept of good, and the distribution of natural abilities. Rawls writes that "Ideally a just constitution would be a just procedure arranged to insure a just outcome."[5] Thus, there is the need to design a just procedure where the liberties of equal citizenship will be incorporated into and protected by the Constitution. For Rawls, these liberties include, among other things, liberty of person and equal political rights. Rawls assumes that in framing a just constitution, the two principles of justice will set the standard for the desired outcome.

Rawls's next point is the legislative stage. The statutes to be enacted must satisfy both the principles of justice and whatever limits are established in the constitution. At this stage, Rawls indicates that the representative legislator does not know the particulars about himself. In concluding his schema, Rawls maintains the primacy of the first principle of justice. He notes that "The first principle of equal liberty is the primary standard for the constitutional convention."[6] The second principle is invoked at the legislative stage. "Thus the priority of the first principle of justice to the second is reflected in the priority of the constitutional convention to the legislative stage."[7]

Before moving to an application of Rawls's theory to children's rights, it will help us to look first at Ronald Dworkin's treatment of Rawls and the interpretation he places on Rawls's concept of justice. Dworkin suggests that Rawls has a "deep theory" and that the underlying fundamental concept of this "deep theory" is the abstract right to equal concern and respect. When Rawls speaks of justice as fairness he means justice to be equal concern and respect. Dworkin argues that the right to equal concern and respect does not emerge from the social contract but is assumed "as the fundamental right must be, in its design."[8] The right is not a product of the contract but a condition of admission to the original position. "This right is 'owed to human beings as moral persons' and follows from the moral personality that distinguishes humans from animals."[9] It is in this light that I will use the theory of justice.

It is important to note that when we discuss Rawls's theory with respect to children's rights that Rawls characterizes rights under his system as "natural," "they are assigned in the first instance to persons and that they are given special weight."[10] Dworkin does not find it disturbing that Rawls makes the right to equal concern and respect natural rather than legal or conventional. He states:

> Justice as fairness rests on the assumption of a natural right of all
> men and women to equality of concern and respect, a right they
> possess not by virtue of birth of characteristic or merit or

41

excellence but simply as human beings with the capacity to make plans and give justice.[11]

In his discussion of Rawls's "deep theory," Dworkin makes the very important distinction (which we will see later has tremendous implications for children) between the right "to equal treatment" and the right "to treatment as an equal." The right to equal treatment is the right to an equal distribution of some opportunity, resource, or burden. The right to treatment as an equal is the right "not to receive the same distribution of some burden or benefit, but to be treated with the same respect and concern as anyone else."[12] Dworkin uses equal respect and concern as an abstract right which serves as a constraint on specific rights. This is to say that, normally, where a particular fundamental right has been recognized and granted to a person, that right must be granted equally to everyone else. However, under certain conditions, the basic right of equal respect and concern can permit a justification of *unequal treatment.* The conditions or grounds for limiting the definition of a right are these: (1) Where the values protected by the original right are not really at stake, (2) situations in which, if the right is defined to include the marginal case, then some competing right (in the strong sense described by Dworkin) would be abridged. (3) where the cost to society would not be simply incremental, if the right were so defined, but would be of a degree far beyond the cost paid to grant the original right, a degree great enough to justify whatever assault on dignity or equality might be involved in withholding the right in the specific case.[13]

While the second and third grounds are important, they are not applicable to the issues being discussed at present. We will be concerned with only the first ground.

In Chapter 3, it was shown that adult patients have certain rights, particularly the right to consent to or refuse medical treatment. This right presupposes the value of making a rational and autonomous decision. In the discussion to follow, I argue that, except in those cases where the first ground can be invoked to limit the right, equal respect and concern requires that children be granted the identical rights afforded to adults — the right to consent to and refuse medical treatment. In these rights, both at law and in ethics, the primary value at stake is rationality. However, if the value of rationality and making a rational decision is not available (that is, it is absent), then under the first ground there is a justification for unequal treatment, a denial to children (as well as incompetent adults) of the right to consent to and refuse medical treatment.

In his explanation of the distinction between the right to equal treatment and the right to treatment as an equal, Dworkin uses the example that if I have two children, one of whom is dying from a terminal disease and that the disease is making the other child uncomfortable, I would not manifest equal concern if I flipped a coin to determine which child should receive the remaining dose of medicine. If we supply some additional data to Dworkin's example, we can demonstrate more fully the relationship between the right to treatment as an equal and the right to equal treatment, as well as an understanding of a justification of *unequal treatment.* Suppose the dying child is a 5-year-old boy and is experiencing a fair amount of pain, while the other child is a 14-year-old girl. We can also suppose that the medicine to be given, of which there is only one dose remaining, is a pain-relieving drug. By looking at the expanded case, we can see that unequal treatment cannot be justified because of the sex of the children, or their ages. These factors clearly are not the values at stake in the administration of the medicine. Likewise, if it were involved, race would not be a value at stake and would not justify unequal treatment. I would suggest, however, that there are some factors apart from sex, age, and race which, when properly examined in light of the first ground, could justify unequal treatment. The intensity of pain being experienced by two patients is one such factor. Thus, in the expanded example, the pain of the dying child could justify unequal treatment. Another factor which is more directly related to the discussion to follow could be the patient's inability to make a rational decision, thus justifying a denial to the patient of the opportunity to consent to the proposed treatment.

In applying Dworkin's interpretation of Rawls's deep theory to the subject at hand — the rights of children in treatment for catastrophic and mental illnesses — it seems (*prima facie* at least) that there can be no distinguishing features in the exercise of rights by children and by adults without considering first the prevailing equality of concern and respect. With this sketch, we can now turn to the implications Rawls's theory holds for children's rights.

II. "THE THEORY" AND CHILDREN

Initially, children are participants in the formation of the initial contract as far as they are capable. The only restriction that Rawls assigns to participants is that one must be *rational* which includes the idea for Rawls that a participant must have attained the "age of reason."[14] Rawls does not attempt to apply a definition of this age, or to connect it to a specific idea of rationality and understanding. This fact is important when I discuss later separation of a preconceived concept of rationality and understanding from the chronological age and development of a child. There is room in Rawls's view for the implication that a child's participation should grow as his or her competencies develop.

What is of first importance to Rawls is the actual capacity for accepting the principle of fairness and whether or not this capacity that has developed is secondary. He writes, "A being that has this capacity, whether or not it is yet developed, is to receive the full protection of the principle of justice."[15]

It would seem at least, that those children born with the capacity to ultimately develop an acceptance of the principle of fairness are participants with just claims of fair treatment. This is not enough, however, for by itself the capacity criterion eliminates those children who might have lost the capacity because of mental illness or never possessed the capacity in the first place, as in the case of a profoundly retarded newborn. Coupled with this inability to ever develop the capacity is the conflicting issue of paternalism through parental domination; parental domination that could be expected to exist for those children who cannot fully participate in the initial social contract for whatever reason.

Rawls deals carefully with this question and the reality of children and others whom society must treat paternally. It is the veil of paternalism that must be lifted and understood if Rawls's theory is to provide the moral framework for allowing children's rights.

Rawls argues that lack of full participation by children in the initial social contract *does not lead* to a justification for parental domination. This position would also take care of the child who is mentally unable to perform rationally.[16] It is Rawls's position that those choosing in the original position of society are choosing not only for themselves but for all who are to come. This thesis has tremendous implications for children's rights. The original participants *must choose* principles without being aware of their age or generation, besides not knowing their status situation. In doing this, then, the participants must accept the possibility of being children, or even of being unborn. Any choices concerning principles of justice must be made with this contingency in mind.

Rawls feels that the participants in the original position would probably agree to paternalism in some form. He writes:

> Others are authorized and sometimes required to act on our behalf and to do that what we would do for ourselves if we were rational, this authorization coming into effect only when we cannot look after our own good. Paternalistic decisions are to be guided by the individual's own settled preferences and interests insofar as they are not irrational, or failing a knowledge of these, by the theory of primary goods. As we know less and less about a person, we act for him as we would act for ourselves from the standpoint of the original position. We try to get for him the things he presumably wants whatever else he wants. We must be able to argue that with the development in question will accept our decision on his behalf and agree with us that we did the best thing for him.[17]

It would seem that those consenting to paternalism in the original position would be extremely reluctant to select any rigid form of paternalism and one which did not offer some protection against abuses of authority by members of the older generation. In addition, the interests of the child are not necessarily synonymous with those of parents or protectors.

Under the framework of Rawls's theory, where the principles of justice are applied, paternalistic intervention would not deprive or negate children's rights. Without question, there are specific situations involving medical matters, for example, in the case of the very young or profoundly retarded, where paternalistic decisions are necessary in order to provide "primary goods"; however, even there, three conditions must be met and followed before paternalistic intervention is permitted; conditions which are applicable in all cases involving minors. They also provide the basis for recognizing identical moral rights in all children regardless of age: A congruity which is not recognized at law where the "age of reason" is to some extent arbitrarily chronologically established. In the discussion to follow, as we consider specific rights (such as the right to consent or refuse treatment), the three conditions will be employed to either justify or deny the expression of a right.

The first condition is the presumption of rationality in all persons. As previously stated, Rawls suggests that the participants (who are acting for those unborn, and for all to come) would probably agree to paternalism in some form. Those participating fully in the formation of the initial social theory must have attained the "age of reason."

It is important to stop for a moment and point out that Rawls's conception of rationality can be separated into two distinct presumptions: as a meta-ethical principle and as a normative principle. In the first case, the meta-ethical (which is not directly involved in my conclusions), Rawls is not speaking of a genuine presumption of rationality but rather a "procedural presumption" that is hypothetical in nature. As Ronald Green adeptly points out, rationality is the necessary factor for a person to be a member of the moral community. He writes, "The understanding of morality conditions the nature of the moral choice procedure and finally determines who is permitted to participate in the procedure and enjoy its benefit."[18]

In the second case (which my discussion now involves), Rawls moves to establish the normative requirements for his principle of the presumption of rationality. This principle can be compared with the principle of the presumption of innocence that prevails in American and English criminal jurisprudence. The presumption stands by itself. A person does not have to prove he is innocent. Instead, the burden of overcoming the presumption rests with the state in all cases. The same can be said to be true of the presumption of rationality. One does not have to prove his rationality and the burden of disproving it rests with the challenger. It is reasonable to accept the thesis that justice as equal respect and concern would provide for a presumption of rationality in everyone, young and old alike. Under the principles of justice the concept of equal respect and concern could hardly be defended if the presumption of rationality was assigned only to some participants while being denied to others. Thus, before any paternalistic intervention can be justified, the presumption of rationality must be rebutted and overcome. Rawls hints at this in his statement. "Paternalistic intervention must be justified by the evident failure or absence of reason and will."[19]

This condition shifts the burden from proving a particular ethical right by the minor, to those who would deny to children the exercise of their own rights. The presumption of rationality within the principle of equal respect and concern means that each individual has full ability to decide for himself unless the contrary is shown to be just. In the law, by contrast, the presumption of rationality is connected to the concept of adulthood. The inconsistency and unfairness of this can be seen in that a person who had been a minor at age 18 before the age of majority was lowered from 21 to 18, possessed no legal presumption of rationality. Yet, by legislative act — lowering the age of majority to 18 — the presumption of rationality followed and was established.

If the presumption of rationality is unwarranted and overcome, it is then fair to act on one's behalf through paternalistic intervention. It is here that the second condition suggested by Rawls comes into play — the paternalistic intervention must be directed by the child's more permanent goals and desires, or by the consideration of primary goods. "Guided by the principles of justice and what is known about the subject's more permanent aims and preferences, or by the account of primary goods."[20]

Thus, once paternalistic intervention is justified because of a failure of the first condition — the presumption of rationality — at the very minimum, under the second condition, the child-patient should be consulted about his or her aims and preferences. There are exceptions to this condition, as in the case of non-communicative minors (e.g., baby, autistic child, etc.), but they are not fatal to the soundness of the condition when taken into consideration with the third condition.

The third condition, when properly considered, helps provide the essential guarantee that the paternalistic conduct will not be an isolated act that is unrelated to the patient's uniqueness as an individual. Rawls writes:

> We must be able to argue that with the development or the recovery of his rational powers the individual in question will accept our decision on his behalf and agree with us that we did the best thing for him.[21]

Thus, once an agent sets out on a paternalistic decision-making course on behalf of a minor patient, the decisions made must be acceptable decisions — acceptable in the sense that if and when he possessed rationality, he would recognize and accept the decisions as being the best thing for him at the time.[22]

It is time now to turn to a consideration of the relationship between Rawls's theory and the legal rights as discussed in Chapter 3, and specific ethical rights which may or may not be compatible with the existing legal position of minor's rights.

III. "THE THEORY" AND LEGAL RIGHTS

In my discusssion of legal rights, the existence and expression of minor's rights were found to be based either upon legislative origin or judicial decision. In either case, the ultimate guarantee of the constitutional right of privacy was relied upon.

It was also shown that constitutional dimensions have been accorded to two principles: parental control and *parens patriae*. At times these two principles conflict with the right of privacy and, depending on the nature of the case, either override the right or are subservient to it. There is, however, a common element present in all three, which tends to serve as the connecting factor between them. This element might be referred to as the legal rationale for according and denying to minors their rights, but it is akin to the philosophical rationale explicated in my discussion of Rawls. I am speaking of the "presumption of rationality" and "capacity to choose."

The concept of rationality and capacity to choose is a critical element in any legal theory of rights and in most ethical theories. In American jurisprudence, the absence of "capacity to choose" supports the invocation of the principles of parental control and *parens patriae*. While the right to privacy is not founded upon the presumption of rationality and capacity to choose, but rather a constitutional right extended to "persons,"[23] enforcement of the right and recognition of the constellation of rights rooted in "privacy" (i.e., right to consent, informed consent) are deferred to parental control and *parens patriae* where capacity is totally lacking or diminished.

As demonstrated earlier, state restrictions inhibiting privacy rights of minors are valid only if they tend to serve some significant state *interest*. The interest, though limited, is based in part upon the contention that a child is not possessed of "that full capacity for individual choice."

In the case of *parens patriae*, the burden of justifying restraints upon the freedom of minors is placed squarely on the state and the state must demonstrate clearly and continuously a lack of "full capacity." We can find support in Rawls's theory here in that all persons, children and adults alike, are granted constitutional guarantee of privacy — that is, all things being equal (i.e., capacity) rights afforded adults are equally afforded to minors. At least at this level the concept of justice as equal respect and concern is present.

Rawls also provides for paternalistic intervention where "capacity to

47

choose" is missing. This intrusion on the privacy of an individual and his self-autonomy is only permitted when the presumption of rationality has been overridden. Rawls does not restrict a paternalistic intervention to cases involving children, but provides for its employment to all persons who demonstrably no longer possess rationality. Paternalistic intervention's legal counterpart is through the doctrines of *parens patriae* and parental control.

In keeping with Rawls' theory, *parens patriae* is not restricted to minors, but is used consistently by the state in assuming control of the affairs of adults who have clearly shown that they no longer possess presumption of rationality and "capacity to choose." It should be recognized though that a minor's presumption of rationality and capacity to choose is *prima facie* dismissed by the state in many cases through legislative acts. I am speaking of public laws that are directed singularly at minors as distinguished from adults — for example, the age of consent to sexual relations. There would appear to be a break in the concept of equal· respect and concern in that an adult's "capacity to choose" is not touched by such legislative acts. However, a minor in reality still possesses the presumption of capacity and can, by contesting the constitutionality of the particular act, force the state to a judicial determination to demonstrate its absence.

The principle of parental control is different, though, because historically the traditional concept of "family" permits the determination of the minor's capacity by the parent. This suggests that "presumption of rationality" and "capacity to choose" are not present in children; or else that a minor is permitted to choose or decide only in those things sanctioned by his or her parent. At each stage of the child's development, the parent makes the decision to override the "presumption." The enlightened parent will recognize the presumption of rationality and will weigh the degree to which rationality is present at each stage in the development of the child.

The court has on occasion pierced the family shield when the privacy right of the child was so paramount that the family or state should not overcome the child's capacity to choose.An example of this can be seen in the cases cited on abortion and the use of contraceptives without parental permission.[24]

It would seem then that Rawls has room for *parens patriae* and in a guarded sense parental control. The main difference, however, separating Rawls and the legal system is that legally the presumption of rationality and "capacity to choose" is connected to the chronological development of children and in all but a few isolated cases (right to privacy) no amount of proof is permitted to demonstrate the capacity to choose. In the final analysis, the legal methodology employed for overcoming the "presumption" is directly connected to age. It is this element that separates the legal from the ethical in the exercise of rights in medical matters. In those cases cited, where the court has looked beyond the chronological factor and solicited the opinion of the minor, the Rawlsian concept of justice as fairness has been employed (though not explicitly).

Rawls's theory seems to support those specific decisions which allow for parallel expressions of rights in minors and adults. For example, the principle is manifested in the application of the right to privacy to minors and adults alike in the decision-making process of abortion. Other examples are the right to purchase contraceptives, emergency treatment, and the concept of informed consent.

Thus, Rawls's theory provides an ethical framework for supporting those specific decisions which recognize some expression of children's rights. It is the concept of justice as equal respect and concern for *all* "persons" that provides the underlying theme for postulating the principle of identical rights — that children's rights are *prima facie* identical to adult rights. Equal respect and concern assumes the universality of a presumption of rationality in every person and hence, does not permit any distinction between expressions of rights by minors and adults until that presumption is overcome.

Because of the tremendous moral force of this principle, the complexities surrounding child and adult rights give way to a singular understanding of adult rights. In all cases, apart from a negation of the "presumption of rationality," there is no designated "adult" right or "child" right; they are simply one and the same. Only when an individual's rationality has been diminished to the extent that it overrides a presumption of its presence is any withdrawal of rights permitted along with a paternalistic intervention. Even then, as we will see, equal respect and concern remains a constant condition throughout the ensuing paternalistic action.

Before turning to a discussion of specific ethical rights, we should have some understanding of "rationality" as I will use it throughout the remainder of my essay. For Rawls, individuals are rational in the sense that they can recognize their own interests, that their interests can be coherently ordered, and that if they need to they can postpone immediate gratification for the sake of their long run interests as they conceive them. It is the phrase "that their interests can be coherently ordered" which in the end clearly establishes rationality.

Rawls states, "At any give time rational persons decide between plans of action in view of their situation and beliefs, all in conjunction with their present desires and the principles of rational choice."[25] We choose between future desires in the light of existing desires; and, when an individual determines what he wants to be, he adopts a particular plan of life. Rawls includes among one's existing desires the desire to act on rational principles. It will help us later if we briefly look at Rawls' explication of rational principles, since he suggests that they are to replace the concept of rationality.

One principle of rational choice is that of postponement. We can delay immediate gratification for the sake of a long run interest. A second principle is that of effective means. For Rawls, this principle is perhaps the most natural criterion of rational choice. Simply put, if we are to suppose that there is an end objective that we desire, and that all the alternatives are means to gain it, then we are to choose that plan which accomplishes the end in the best way. Rawls states, "Given the objective, one is to achieve it with the least expenditure of means (whatever they are); or given the means, one is to fulfill the objective to the fullest possible extent."[26]

Rawls also states, "This principle is perhaps the most natural criterion of rational choice."[27] The effective means are coherently structured, insofar as possible, to attain the life goal.

A third principle is that of inclusiveness. This principle indicates that we should follow the plan that would best achieve all of the desired aims of it as well as any other plan. Alternative plans will not always exist; but where they do, we are to follow the more inclusive plan. The rationale behind this principle is that by adopting the inclusive plan we will realize a much wider set of ends, while at the same time, leaving nothing undone that might have been accomplished by the other plan.

A final principle is that of the greater likelihood. In some situations two plans might be roughly the same. When this exists we might determine that more of our objectives are likely to be fulfilled by one plan than the other. We are to follow the plan then that promises to be the most rewarding of our end objectives.

Rawls adds to the principles discussed the concept of "deliberative rationality" which is particularly applicable to cases within a medical context. A rational plan for a person, in addition to being consistent with the principles mentioned, is one that is chosen with deliberative rationality. This is to say that rationality in decision-making includes a careful reflection on all of the relevant facts and what it might be like to carry out one's plans and the course of action necessary to best realize the end result. Rawls assumes that the deciding agent is under no misconception as to what he really wants in life and that, "In most cases anyway, when he achieves his aim, he does not find that he no longer wants it and wishes that he had done something else instead."[28] Firmness of commitment is involved here.

It is essential that the deciding agent's knowledge of his situation and the consequences of carrying out his plan be presumed to be correct and complete. This entails that he be fully informed of all of the relevant circumstances insofar as possible. I have added to Rawls's definition of rationality an important feature which I believe is necessary to any consideration of the role it plays in decision-making — especially decision-making in medical matters. The concept of rationality includes a realistic understanding of one's true medical and mental state in relation to the surrounding world. Thus, not only should the patient be fully apprised of necessary information for a rational decision, there must be, in addition, a connection between his understanding of this information and his understanding of its relation to the surrounding world.

As a concluding thought on rationality, Charles Fried seems to tie together neatly the concept of rationality and coherently ordered interests. Fried suggests that for interests to be coherently ordered there must be a coherence and consistency between ends, attitude, emotions, and relations. The rational actor has a sense of deeper understanding of his own ends and values; he is "conscious" of the ordering of the constituent elements of his end — he consciously orders the elements in accordance with the life plan, or rules, principles which are necessary to that end.[29]

This concept of rationality will be demonstrated in the case studies to follow and the child studies which are cited.

IV. "THE THEORY" AND ETHICAL RIGHTS

"Consent Rights"

"Consent rights" (i.e., right to consent to treatment, informed consent, refusal of treatment) are perhaps the most fundamental of our legal and ethical rights in medical matters. Because they rest upon the basic principle of self-determination over one's own body, support from Rawls's ethical framework for existing legal positions can perhaps be more readily observed here than in other cases. Insofar as adults are concerned the picture of legal and ethical rights is clear. The existing legal position is simply a restatement of the ethical principle of self-determination — that every human being of adult years and sound mind has a right to determine what shall be done with his or her own body.[30]

A more explicit statement which embraces the principle of equal respect and concern appears in the leading case of *Natanson v. Kline.*

> Anglo-American law starts with the premise of thorough going self-determination. It follows that each person is considered to be master of his own body, and he/she may, if he/she be of sound mind, expressly prohibit the performance of life-saving surgery, or other medical treatment. A doctor might well believe that an operation or form of treatment is desirable or necessary but the law does not permit him to substitute his own judgment for that of the patient by any form of artifice or deception.[31]

This position is a restatement of adult rights to consent to and refuse medical treatment previously set forth and discussed in Chapter 3. Only when we turn to the application of the consent principle to children do the basic legal and ethical principles become incongruous.

To begin with, the principle of identical rights does not permit any arbitrary determination of "consent rights" based on the chronological development of children. The necessary presence of the presumption of rationality in all persons precludes any blanket dismissal in children of the right to consent to or refuse medical treatment. Equal respect and concern means that every medical case must be considered on an individual basis, and *prima facie* at least, consent or refusal to the performance of some treatment rests in the individual whether an adult or a minor. We cannot simply intervene paternalistically and dismiss with a wave of the hand a minor's request to withdraw treatment, without first successfully challenging his presumption of rationality.

The law, of course, does not recognize *prima facie* or otherwise any rights "to consent" in children, especially consent rights for children in treatment for catastrophic illnesses. The exceptions to the position (i.e., right to abort) are based upon an extension of the constitutional right of privacy. However, ethical support for consent rights can be drawn from the principle of equal respect and concern because the court in recognizing the right in children employed the standard of adult persons. One can assume an acceptance of continuing "rationality" in the children involved since it was not an issue before the court as in the *Ginsburg* case.[32] However, these exceptions do not deal with the subject at hand — children in treatment for catastrophic illnesses. As a general rule the courts have failed to apply equal respect and concern because the attainment of "adult rights" by children is based on their chronological development. Paternalistic intervention either by the principle of parental control or *parens patriae* is exercised without any regard to the concept of rationality.

Thus, the task before us now is to examine the strengths and weaknesses of the "presumption" of rationality and the ease and difficulty with which it can and cannot be rebutted. In pursuing this task, I believe it will greatly help us to challenge and defend the "presumption" with the use of specific medical cases. We will see (not unexpectedly) with advancement in a child's age and moral development, the presumption of rationality becomes harder to refute and ultimately cannot be distinguished from that of an adult's.

The easiest and most obvious starting point is the very young — the minor from one-day-old up to five years. It is unlikely here that the presumption of rationality can withstand a simple cursory examination. While the young infant or the three or five-year-old child might recognize and be aware of their own interests, as they understand them, it is highly improbable that they possess a deep understanding of their ends and values to the extent that they can be coherently ordered in relation to those ends and values. For example, a three-year-old child's rejection of chemotherapy for leukemia will not be based upon any concept of the statistical relationship between the proposed treatment and prolongation of life (or an extended quality of life), but because he is frightened of it or "it makes him feel bad." Certainly the latter are real interests but the child can only understand and act on these interests in a narrow sense.[33] While his interests are important, for there to be rationality, these interests must be coherently ordered in the sense that they produce a coherence or consistency with a selected rational life plan. Even though a child might very well have begun to imagine and to verbally affirm what he would like to be when he grows up, it is doubtful that his plan has been selected with the "deliberative rationality" Rawls suggests as necessary to make a rational life plan. Thus, little argument can be offered to the proposition that the very young cannot withstand a challenge to the presumption of rationality. We can conclude that they do not possess identical rights with adults in the consenting to or refusing medical treatment.

However, as previously posited, once the presumption of rationality is overcome and paternalistic intervention is proper (ethically valid), two other necessary conditions must be satisfied — the paternalistic intervention must be directed by the child's more permanent goals and interests and that the decisions made on his behalf must be such that the child will with development of rationality accept them as the best thing for him. In the case of the three-year-old child, the paternalistic agent must, before making a decision to either accept or reject chemotherapy for him, counsel with the child as to his discernible interests and goals and what the proposed course of treatment will or will not do in relation to those expressed interests. It should be made clear that the attempt to learn and understand the interests of the child is not restricted to verbal communication. Indeed, other reliable methods such as behavioral observance should be employed. What is necessary is that, insofar as possible, the interests of the child should be recognized and connected to the decision-making process. It might appear ridiculous or even ludicrous to talk with children at such an early age or to observe them for their interests and goals, but it is necessary to the integrity of what is being argued here.

If communication with the child is open, every effort should be made by the agent to coordinate interests so that there will be as much agreement as possible between the agent and the child in the direction the course of treatment will take. In any event, whether the paternalistic agent's decision is contrary to the child's or in agreement with it, the action taken must be based at all times upon equal respect and concern which dictates in the end that the child (once having acquired rationality) will accept the action as the best thing for him. It is this last condition which is the critical factor in the application of "equal respect and concern," and which in the end ultimately validates any paternalistic intervention. Even though the act of intervening with the self-autonomy of a person is initially ethically valid (because of the absence of the presumption of rationality), the child has the ethical right that the last condition will be fulfilled; that the intervention will be a continuous ethical act from its inception to its conclusion.

The principle of equal respect and concern underscores the thesis that every patient is unique and therefore every medical decision affecting that patient is unique. If the patient's autonomy has been overridden by paternalistic intervention, the uniqueness of the decision must be maintained by the intruding agent. This uniqueness dictates the necessary condition that the medical decision be "acceptable" to the patient when his rationality is developed or restored. It is plausible to assume that two rational patients might decide on two different courses of treatment for identical illnesses, given their unique attitudes, emotions, goals, etc. Thus, the ultimate decision to be reached then becomes of primary importance, more so than who is to be the paternalistic agent. The latter is important only in the sense that an "acceptable" decision might be more likely realized through actions of one agent rather than another.

In most cases the paternalistic agent will be the parent because the special relationship of parent-child provides the basis for a sense of understanding the interests and desires of the child which is not found in other relationships. If the parent is fully informed as to the nature of the illness, alternative courses of treatment, and prognosis for recovery (disability or death), it is likely an "acceptable" decision will be reached. This is not without exception though. Because a parent's self-interests must be reconciled with the decision to be made, these interests must not interfere with the rightness of the decision if the intervention is to be maintained as an ethical act. The emotional make-up of a parent when a child is critically ill, or certain religious beliefs and practices (i.e., Jehovah's Witnesses) can easily diminish the decision-making capacity of a parent and interfere with an "acceptable" decision.

It will be helpful here if we look at the following three cases to demonstrate how important it is that the agent's decision be "acceptable."

Case 1. Jim Pawley, a five-year-old, was on a summer vacation with his parents, two older brothers, and a younger sister. They were driving to a cabin in the country when they were involved in a head-on automobile accident. The father and two older brothers were killed. Jim's leg was pinned in the wrecked automobile, breaking the femur in two places and crushing some of the thigh muscle. After spending several months hospitalized, the orthopedist recommended corrective surgery. With the operation Jim would have an excellent chance of complete recovery of the function of the leg. Without the operation there was a 90% chance he would lose complete use of the leg for life. The only risk in the operation was from the general anesthesia which had a statistical basis of one death in two thousand.

Jim's mother, who also was in the accident, but had escaped serious injury had not recovered completely from the trauma of the death of her husband and two children. She had become deeply religious following the accident and prayed every morning and evening for her son's recovery. When she was approached by the doctor for permission to perform corrective surgery, she refused permission saying, "God's will be done." She also expressed concern over minimal risk of endangering her son's life with the operation. When the young boy was consulted about his interest, he expressed agreement with his mother.[34]

For the purposes of discussion and to move to the issue of acceptablity, we can assume in this case that Jim's presumption of rationality has been overcome and a paternalistic intervention would be proper. The child has been consulted as to his interests and desires and the only question remaining is the "acceptability" of the medical decision to be made — whether or not to perform the corrective surgery. The question to ask is this: Will Jim, when he is 18 years of age, accept the denial of corrective surgery and the loss of the use of his leg for life, when the operation would have resulted in only minimal residual disability?

The right of the child to a paternalistic decision which is later acceptable to him carries with it the corresponding right that the agent refrain at all times from including his own self interest in the decision-making process and attempt to be objective. Objectivity here means a disengagement from one's own self-attitudes, emotions, personal goals, religious beliefs, etc. It does not carry the meaning that the same decision will be reached in those cases that are based on identical medical history. To do so would deny the uniqueness of each patient that is so essential in the application of "equal respect and concern." There is no question though that in many cases, such as the one being discussed, the same "acceptable" decision will ordinarily be reached. There is no identifiable *permanent* interest of Jim's that dictates avoiding the risk of surgery. A medical prognosis is derived from a study of medical histories that have produced identical results from a particular course of treatment.

Thus, in this case, because the mother is deeply involved emotionally and cannot realistically grasp an appraisal of the medical prognosis for her son if the corrective surgery is not performed, the child has the right to a paternalistic agent other than his mother. It should be noted that just as the right to life of an unconscious patient does not have to be expressed in order to be valid, the child's right to an acceptable decision through a neutral agent does not have to be claimed. The neutral agent can be a patient's advocate who will represent the child under sanction of law, or the case could be handled through direct intervention of the state by *parens patriae* as in the blood transfusion cases.[35] While generally adult Jehovah's Witnesses are permitted legally to refuse blood for themselves even if refusal is tantamount to death, they cannot refuse blood transfusions for their children. The legal principle is upheld in the Supreme Court's

55

statement that "Right to practice religious freedom freely does not include the liberty to expose a child to ill health or death."[36] The court's position is not necessarily compatible with the ethical framework being advanced here. It does not take into consideration the desires and goals of the child or the acceptability of the decision by him. A child might upon developing rationality, choose to adhere to the religious discipline expected of him as a Jehovah's Witness and forego a blood transfusion.

Case 2. The second type of case involves a dying "young child." At first glance it might appear that cases involving the voiceless patient (i.e., baby, retarded person) present few problems. Direct communication with the patient concerning his interests and goals is certainly eliminated; however, this does not mean that the intervening agent is free to impose his interest upon the patient or not to consciously inquire within himself as to what those interests might be. In the case where surgery is necessary to save the life of a six-day-old baby with Down's Syndrome, the agent's decision to refuse surgery and permit the baby to die can find moral support within my thesis, though legal support is lacking. If the paternalistic agent is informed as to the nature of Down's Syndrome and the ultimate prognosis for the baby, the baby's interest and goals for life should be fairly discernible and an "acceptable" decision made. It is highly improbable that once a person's rationality has developed in such a case (hypothetically only) that he would select to live hopelessly retarded and institutionalized for life.

I am well aware that the last statement is controversial and that arguments have been offered to the effect that some Down's Syndrome children appear to be quite happy. The point being made is, however, that a rational person would be aware of a far greater dimension to life than that offered to the retarded child, and knowing this, he would rather forego the surgery necessary to save his life.

It is another matter though when the situation involves a dying child who can communicate and whose interest at the time might be counter to his parents and the physicians.

Case 3. Peter was an extremely bright 7-year-old boy. His reading ability was that expected at sixth grade level. He took an active interest in current events and could engage in a fairly sophisticated conversation on worldly topics. Peter was suffering from leukemia which had been diagnosed when he was three years old. For the past four years he had been an "in and out" patient at a cancer research hospital undergoing, under various protocols, extensive chemotherapy and radiation therapy. Peter was dying now and had been placed on a respirator. He was resting comfortably and had a clear mind. He was able to talk at length with his mother and friends about dying and had read during the past weeks two books on dying. From reading these books, Peter had developed his own philosophical understanding of death and a religious belief in what kind of death it would be. He was "absolute" in his belief that death would free him from the intense pain and general discomfort he was now experiencing. The doctors had approached Peter's mother with a new protocol which carried little promise beyond simple hope that a remission period could be established. The new protocol was not discussed with Peter. Shortly before the protocol was to begin, Peter summoned his mother to his bedside and told her that he was ready to die, that "he was not afraid of death ", and "that death would carry a release from his pain." His mother then told him of the protocol and asked Peter to consider the new hope for some temporary cure. In response, Peter explained in depth the state he would be in when he was dead and that it would have the dimension of joy and freedom from pain which was missing in his life now. He then asked that the respirator be turned off and that he be allowed to die. After a few minutes of thought his mother asked him if this was what he really wanted and after an explicit yes, she turned the respirator off and permitted Peter to die in her arms.[37]

In some cases involving dying children, the parents and medical staff may want the struggle against death to continue in hopes of a miraculous cure or a new medical drug. They argue emotionally that a new experimental protocol might provide the cure though hope is virtually non-existent. This position by itself is not ethically wrong. Parental interests are not without value, and there is always the remote possiblity that a new protocol might produce a remission of the disease and permit an extension of life. However, in the case of the dying child, we are not dealing primarily with parental concerns although they are important. The central issue is the right of the child to consent to further chemotherapy or to terminate all life-support measures. It is the ethical act of the paternalistic agent that is on stage, and the presumption of rationality with its unique relationship to every patient must be dealt with on an individual basis. Even though studies indicate that a child at ages 5-7 confuses myth and reality and cannot relate to others meaningfully, the ability of the child to clearly discern what is happening to him, as in Peter's case, cannot be taken lightly. From my observations of dying children in a major research hospital, I am convinced that a 7-year-old child has a firmer grasp on the reality of his situation than might generally be understood and his decision to be let along or to forego any further radical treatment, painfully excruciating to him, is in most cases firmly based upon a sense of impending death. A sensitive child may learn from his body information about his prognosis not available to anyone else.

Thus, while parental interest is not without value, the right of the young child to request a termination of his treatment can be dealt with and supported within the principle of equal respect and concern. The acceptability of the decision to terminate treatment is paramount to its ethical validity. The paternalistic agent must consider the fact that a fully rational child (if rationality has been dismissed) might ratify his present desire to no longer prolong his life. Anything less would seem to negate the ethical validity of any paternalistic intervention on behalf of the child.

It might be argued that Peter's situation is an exception to the rule, that most 7-year-old children are not in possession of the moral and rational development he demonstrated. This might be true but such an argument misses the main thrust of the principle of equal respect and concern — that there can be no arbitrary assignment of rationality; each case must be considered on its individual merits. What should be recognized is, as studies have shown, that moral reasoning and development begins its transition from heteronomy to autonomy in 6-10-year-old children and the possibility of a rational agent exists. At these ages the child is becoming more of a social creature. He is exposed to more of the real world through school, home and play; and his concept of death and death's relationship to causes such as disease is more fixed. More than a cursory inquiry is necessary to overcome the presumption of rationality in the case of a 7-year-old.[38]

It is when we turn to the 11-16-year-old adolescent that the principle of identical rights makes it strongest offering. The presumption of rationality is more firmly fixed and the uniqueness of every patient must be carefully considered in any attempt to overcome the presumption. The capacity-incapacity issue is not as clear as the law supposes. In fact, the capacity of the minor for rational decision-making is far greater then the law allows. There is substantial agreement among child psychologists and sociologists that the moral and intellectual maturity of the 13-year-old approaches that of the adult. Persons generally reach their adult levels of abstract intelligence and moral development long before the termination of childhood, at around puberty. For about the last 8 years or so of infancy (10-18), a person has about as much capacity to exercise choice as an adult. Recent studies on the capacity-incapacity issue strongly suggest that the middle years child possesses an ever-broadening field of general knowledge which permits him to think in ways that come to approximate those of adults.[40] Indeed, in some areas, the child may know a great deal more than his parents and so be able to think more rationally than they. In their studies on childhood and adolescence, Joseph Stone and Joseph Church indicate that the world of the middle-years child includes isolated domains or segments of experience which are logically organized and about which the child can reason in a mature fashion. By the years of 12 and 13, the child has experienced a dramatic change of quality of reasoning, and the use of reason, he possesses self-awareness and has judgmental abilities. He can with clarity imagine possibilities and alternatives.[41] It is precisely these areas that must be examined and tested under the thesis of identical rights.

Obviously, intellectual capacity does not in itself qualify as the only criterion for decision making. A person can be irrational and have the intellectual capacity for decision making all at the same time. However, intellectual capacity is a positive factor in determining whether or not a rational decision can be made by a 13-year-old minor. If the child cannot grasp realistically the substance of the medical decision facing him and the alternatives to either accepting the treatment or refusing it, the presumption of rationality would be seriously challenged if not overcome.

The growing maturity of the 13-year-old is reflected in statutes and court decisions that give the young adolescent a voice in matters of custody and marriage. Many states recognize that "choice" of a child between 10 and 14 should be considered as a factor in awarding custody. In the landmark cake of *Wisconsin v. Yoder*[42] Justice Douglas, citing the works of Piaget and other authorities, argues for an even younger age of responsibility than 14 years.[43] The state of New York has recently enacted a new law which provides that a 13-year-old can have the capacity for moral responsibility. I am employing the support of these authorities, not to establish a general case for adolescent rationality, but rather to demonstrate that some evidence does exist for arguing its existence in any particular case. As the studies and court decisions have suggested, the 13-year-old can and does possess the capacity for rational decision making and this fact cannot be over-looked in the treatment of children for catastrophic illnesses. This line of thought is reflected in the following case study.

Karen is a 13-year-old patient suffering from an irreversible kidney malfunction. She undergoes thrice-weekly hemodialysis. Karen has recently undergone a second unsuccessful kidney transplant. She tolerates her dialysis poorly, and routinely experiences heavy chilling, nausea, vomiting, severe headaches and weakness. After having been informed that her kidneys would never function, Karen expressed the wish to stop medical treatment and let "nature take its course."

The attending medical staff said such wishes were unheard of and unacceptable. Three weeks later the arteriovenous shunt placed in Karen's arm for hemodialysis was found to be infected, and part of the vein wall was excised and the shunt revised. Karen continued to express the wish to discontinue the treatment. Four days later the shunt clotted closed and Karen, with her parents' support, refused shunt revision and any further dialysis. What is very important to note is that during this time Karen prepared a will and selected a burial spot located near her favorite horseback riding trail and home. She displayed a clear awareness of her impending death and her wish to stop all treatment. She told her father, "Daddy, I will be happy there (in the ground) if there is no machine and they don't work on me any more."

For Karen, no medical treatment offered any significant possibility of resuming a life worth living. The medical staff's decision to continue prolongation of Karen's life was a moral judgment rather than a scientific

59

one. It was not a judgment directed at overcoming Karen's presumption of rationality, the initial condition necessary for disregarding the principle of identical rights. It is interesting to note that had Karen been an adult, as determined by the law's chronological scale, the medical staff would have had to terminate the treatment.

Even though — in the end — no challenge was offered to Karen's presumption of rationality, we might look at such a challenge to see if it would have been successful. In doing so we should keep in mind the concept of rationality being employed — a coherence and consistency between ends, attitude, emotions and relations that gives to the actor a deeper understanding of his own ends and values. Such coherence and consistency are not only related to the understanding of life plans or goals but to a realistic grasp of the existing situation and its relation to one's own ends and values. This realism includes comprehending the available alternatives and the finality of the decision when made. The empirical data of Karen's case supports the studies previously reported.[44] But what is more important is that Karen's rationality is demonstrated by some simple coherent acts — acts which we would expect a rational adult to perform. After it was clear to Karen that her kidneys would never function again, she expressed a wish to stop all treatment and then prepared for death with a deep understanding of some values that are related to such an end. She prepared a will and selected a burial site. These two acts are highly significant in that they demonstrate Karen's understanding of her medical situation and impending death.[45] It is highly plausible to assume that one would want to put her affairs in order when death is imminent. Just the understanding of the concept of a will is an expression of rationality. The selection of a burial site is an extremely private act and denotes to some degree the body's death and its interment. For Karen, pain would not follow her to her burial site.

A second case presents a different picture, one that makes it more difficult to permit a minor to consent to and refuse medical treatment. Yet, it is one that can be ethically supported by my thesis, in that it offers a convincing argument against a challenge to the presumption of rationality and hence would allow for identical rights.

Mary, age 12, has been diagnosed as having osteosarcoma of the right hip. The recommended treatment is extensive surgery that will involve nearly the entire right side of Mary's body. The operation will leave Mary literally a half-person, reduced to being a wheelchair invalid. The surgery will remove Mary's right leg, hip and a goodly portion of her upper torso to the right shoulder. The prognosis of recovery with this type of radical operation is 40%. Without the operation the prognosis is terminal and she would live at most only another six months.

Mary wants to be a ballerina. She began taking lessons at age six and has taken lessons continuously up until two months ago, at the time when she began experiencing some discomfort in her hip. For the past three years she has been practicing at an average of two hours a day, six days a week. Mary had planned on entering an eastern ballet school when she reached 16 years of age. From the very first day of the medical diagnosis, Mary has continuously inquired as to whether or not her legs will be involved and how her dancing career will be affected. After both she and her parents were informed as to the gravity of her condition, Mary specifically requested to forego the operation and let "nature heal her if it could." She did not want to be confined to a wheelchair as a half-woman regardless of the 40% chance she might live. Both her parents and the doctors have decided that the operation is the only course to take if Mary's life is to be saved.[46]

The two critical issues in Mary's case are: A demonstration of the rational thinking of Mary when under similar medical facts any rational adult would have the right, both legal and moral, to refuse the operation. And, that the decision to operate is one that Mary would accept later on when her rationality developed if it is missing now.

Consistency of a life purpose is clearly manifested in Mary's dedication to a professional career. Studies on child development indicate that it is not uncommon for dedication to life goals to be crystalized in early years of adolescence. To assume that one would not want to live without her legs if her life-desires were focused on the profession of dancing is not irrational. The "rationality" of an act does not assure or require universal acceptance as the right act, though this might be argued by some philosophers. The principle of equal respect and concern allows for each individual's uniqueness and therefore for two entirely different rational acts and consequences among individuals. What is important is not that everyone need agree with Mary's actions, or her "rightness" in decision-making, but that Mary's actions be consistent with the presumption of her rationality. Under such circumstances paternalistic intervention would be unjustifiable. Under the principle of identical rights, Mary would retain the right to control what is done to her body.

The argument might be offered here that Mary could possibly develop an alternative interest in life other than the goal of being a ballerina. This may be true, however, the support of the concept of rationality being employed here does not depend on any possible future development of other goals. The law, of course, in Mary's case would support the principle of family integrity which underscores parental control and would permit the operation. The law, however, has ignored its own inconsistencies in such situations. On the one hand, the rational adult is generally permitted to make the choice of terminating treatment because it is presumed (rightly) that the adult is rational, while on the other hand, the child is denied the choice because it is presumed (unrightly so) that he is irrational until he reaches an arbitrarily determined age. The idea of rationality is simply

61

swept under the rug of family integrity and parental control.

The closest legal parallel to the moral right of children to consent to medical treatment as presented here is the mature minor rule. This rule permits consent to medical care by unemancipated minors of sufficient intelligence to understand the nature and consequences of treatment they are consenting to, where the treatment is for the minor's benefit. This rule has only been applied to minors over the age of 16 and does not consider the right to refuse treatment in situations described in the two cases. Moreover, the rule functions more to protect doctors from charges of battery than to give real consideration to the rights of children.

Before turning to a discussion of other rights, it might be useful now to briefly summarize the moral position of the minor with respect to "consent rights."

1. Under the principle of equal respect and concern, every minor has a *prima facie* right to control what is done to his or her body and hence, the right to informed consent and the right to consent to and refuse medical treatment.

2. The *"prima facie"* consent rights of the minor can be abrogated only by overcoming a strong presumption of rationality.

3. The presumption of rationality is possessed equally by all persons from the moment of birth. The presumption of a one-year-old is no less than that possessed by a 30-year-old person.

4. The presumption can be most easily overcome in the case of the very young child, ages 0-5 years. It becomes increasingly harder from ages 5-10 to overcome such a presumption.

6. The presumption of rationality is extremely difficult to overcome from ages 11 up and careful inquiry is necessary on a case-by-case basis to determine the extent of the capacity to choose.

7. In all cases where the "consent rights" have been abrogated by a valid paternalistic intervention, the patient must be consulted where possible as to his desires, goals and plans in life, and that the ultimate decision be one that he would accept as best for him when (and if) his rationality is developed.

"Other Rights"

The second group of rights belonging to a child are those ethical rights which flow from an individual because of his role as a patient. The minor patient has the *prima facie* right to be recognized as the "primary patient," to control the confidentiality of his medical records, and the right to a patient's advocate of his own choice if possible. It might be argued that these rights are in reality only an extension of the basic consent rights; however, the law treats them individually in judicial deliberations and they merit separate consideration here.

As I set forth in Section IV of Chapter 3 on legal rights, the principle of confidentiality is based upon the special relationship between the patient and his physician or hospital. The nature of this relationship is twofold in that it is founded upon both fiduciary and contractual elements. It is the contractual element which provides the legal basis for classifying a patient as the "primary patient." Thus, even though the fiduciary element is sufficient in itself to provide the legal right of confidentiality to an adult, this right is quickly qualified in the case of a minor because of the absence of the contractual element; the minor does not possess contractual responsibility. Even though the minor becomes the "treated" patient, his parent or guardian, who is the contracting party is the "primary patient." The status of the individual as "primary patient-in-fact" is a very important ethical position. While a contractual element is necessary in a legal relationship, under the principle of equal respect and concern it is *unimportant*.[17] Once the minor patient becomes "primary patient-in-fact" not "pseudo primary patient," all rights accorded an adult in this position are likewise recognized in the minor: the right to control records; the right to change doctors; the right to leave the hospital; etc.

Ethically the contractual element should not be taken into consideration in determining the status of the patient. Equal respect and concern dictates that all treated patients, minors and adults, are primary patients. Under the thesis discussed in the previous section on consent rights, the role can under certain circumstances be enlarged to include the parent, guardian or state as "co-primary patients." The circumstances are those that are conducive to an ethical act of paternalistic intervention. Thus if paternalistic intervention is ethically proper, the agent should be brought into a full physician-patient relationship as a participating partner with the minor.

An ethical and legal argument might be advanced here against my thesis that if the parent, guardian or state is to be held as a responsible party for the medical costs, which they can be, then they should have the final right to control the patient's end of the physician-patient relation ship. They should have access to all records, have the right to release them, etc. (This becomes an even more important argument in the mental illness cases to be discussed later.) An immediate counter-argument is that the law has always recognized that minors were responsible for medical costs. The law has also recognized certain areas of confidentiality where parents do not have access to records, e.g., abortion, treatment for venereal diseases. The better answer, it would seem, is the ethical principle of equal respect and concern. If the presumption of rationality cannot be overcome, then identical rights exist and the minor is entitled to the exclusive role of the "primary patient." Parental responsibility for medical costs is a part of the general legal obligation of child support and maintenance, which can be supported by other ethical arguments. The physician and the hospital have the right to conduct good business and require guarantees for costs, and this is justifiably assessed against the parents as guarantors for their children.

The right to a patient's advocate is a very important right and is one that has gained favor legally in a few states. On the surface it can help assure the patient of a personal surrogate in what is taking place in the hospital. For the most part, the patient's advocate's role in medical hospitals has been restricted to the adult patient. It is the child patient, however, who has the most need for the advocate if his or her right to treatment as an equal is to be recognized. The competent adult patient and the child patient do not begin from the same place in any decision-making process. The legal doctrine of informed consent (among others) separates them. The doctor and hospital must listen to the adult patient and secure his consent, however, it is only out of equity that they might turn to the child patient. The child's right to a patient advocate then is the equalizing factor necessary to assure the child of his voice in matters that pertain to him.

In concluding this section on the rights of children in treatment for catastrophic illnesses, it might be pointed out that there are some adult rights which I have not specifically dealth with, such as the right to be told the truth, the right to hire a lawyer, etc. Any discussion of these rights would simply be *repetitious* in nature. (For example, the right to be told the truth is an essential element in the principle of informed consent and the right to counsel is a constitutional guarantee.) I have focused on the critical rights that separate the adult from the minor and cast the shadow on any serious application of the principle of identical rights.

CHAPTER 5

MENTAL ILLNESS — LEGAL RIGHTS

It is time now to turn to a discussion of the legal and ethical rights of children in treatment for mental illnesses. This is a wide area which is largely uncharted in its scope. To begin with, there is no consensus as to the meaning of 'mental illness' — what it is we mean when we say that a person has a mental illness. An extensive inquiry could be directed to that subject alone.

However, for our purposes, the definition that I have provided in the introduction will suffice—children in treatment for mental illnesses include: *all* children who have been committed or are in the process of being committed to a mental hospital for treatment or custody either voluntarily by parents or guardian, involuntarily by court commitment under *parens patriae*, or through juvenile court commitment in exercise of police powers. This broad definition allows for inclusion of all categories of mental dysfunctions, ranging from the simplest of adolescent reactions to catatonia.

We will be concerned, then, with children who have been admitted to a mental institution for some sort of therapeutic treatment. I have grouped the legal rights to be discussed under nine categories: I. Right to Consent to or Refuse Therapeutic Treatment, II. Right to Counsel and Procedural Due Process, III. Parens Patriae, IV. Juvenile Court Commitments, V. Informed Consent, VI. The Right to Treatment After Commitment, VII. Right Not to be Punished, VIII. Right to Accept or Reject Institutional Labor, and IX. Right to Confidentiality. The structure of my discussion of the law will be similar to that used in the previous two chapters on physical

65

illnesses. Some areas of the discussion will overlap with certain legal points set out in Chapter 3. When this occurs, for the sake of brevity, I will simply make reference to the previous discussion of the point.

There is at this time in most states a distinction between voluntary and involuntary admission of a minor, and important differences in the rights a minor enjoys depend on which side of this distinction he or she falls. This distinction has recently come under legal attack and in the first section on the law I will take up the distinction. I will argue in Chapter 6 on ethics that voluntary hospitalization is virtually non-existent in mental institutions.

I. THE RIGHT TO CONSENT TO OR REFUSE THERAPEUTIC TREATMENT

The right to consent to or refuse treatment in the mental institution is not simply one of choice by the minor. The right as a legal right is contested by a number of other interests such as: parental authority, *parens patriae*, informed consent, procedural due process, and others. These interests sometimes support and sometimes conflict with the minor's right of self-autonomy. Because they are present, they must be dealt with at all times when considering what legal rights a minor possesses in the context of a mental institution and in trying to determine where the law is headed.

The law, both case and statutory, has begun to emancipate some minors to allow them to determine for themselves what health care to pursue.[1] In most states now, 16-year-olds have been granted the right to enter or leave mental institutions over the objections of parents who, in the past, had the authority to arrange for their admission or release as voluntary patients.

The new right to enter or leave mental institutions over the objection of parents is not absolute. It applies only to 16-year-olds and up, and while the statutes provide to a minor the right to give notice of his intent to leave the institution, the law also permits the institution to detain the minor for a period up to 48 hours, during which time a petition can be filed by the parent or state seeking an involuntary commitment.[2] After the petition has been filed, the institution is empowered to detain the minor until the hearing. Thus, while a minor can voluntarily seek to leave the institution, his voluntary status can be altered to that of an involuntary patient.

The hearing on the petition is the same as in the case of an original petition filed for involuntary commitment; however, because the minor is a patient at the time the petition is filed, generally the state's interests are given greater weight under the principle of *parens patriae*. It might be useful to point out that voluntary adult patients who have given notice cannot be detained unless hospital officials convince a court that the patient meets the standards for involuntary commitment (i.e., dangerous to self or others). An involuntarily committed adult patient may seek release in the courts through *habeas corpus* or through the periodic review of commitments which is required by some statutes. The child, however, cannot give notice of an intention to leave if under the age of 16, without approval of the parents who sought the initial commitment, and there are no legal grounds upon which to challenge hospitalization unless the voluntary commitment statutes themselves are challenged. Except by bringing suit on constitutional grounds, the minor patient who seeks discharge has no recourse except to those who agreed to the original hospitalization—his parents and the hospital authorities.[3]

Adherents to the belief in parental control within the family may rely on a long line of Supreme Court decisions dealing with parental-child relationships.[4] The right to family privacy and parental authority, as well as the reciprocal liberty interest of parent and child in the familial bond between them, need no greater justification under the law than that they comport with each state's fundamental constitutional commitment to individual freedom and human dignity.[5]

The Supreme Court has recognized at least two separate parent-child interests as protected by the 14th amendment. One is the entitlement of natural parents and their children to each other, an interest which rests on the fact of biological reproduction and arises when the child is born. The other protected interest is in the familial bonds which develop over time between parents and the children in their long-term care.[6] In the case of *Cleveland Board of Education v. LaFleur*,[7] the court said that the law has a strong presumption in favor of parental authority free from coercive intrusion by agents of the state.

In most states, parents may commit their children to mental institutions without a hearing or any other form of judicial scrutiny. If a parent wants a child committed and a hospital will accept the child as a patient, most legal authorities will not hear the child's protest.[8] If the child will not go voluntarily the parent has the right to seek court commitment of the child as an involuntary patient.[9] Most of the updated statutes provide that a child will not be hospitalized for a period longer than 120 days, at which time his or her case will be reevaluated by a review board. If further treatment is recommended or is necessary, the minor may continue to be hospitalized. This procedure is not necessary where the child has been court committed. Here a revocation of hospitalization can be performed only by the committing court.

II. RIGHT TO COUNSEL AND PROCEDURAL DUE PROCESS

The question of distinguishing between voluntary and involuntary admission of a patient has recently undergone serious scrutiny by the courts with special emphasis on the right to counsel and procedural due process at the time of admission. This interest by the courts extends to the right of a minor to accept or refuse mental therapeutic treatment, at least at the first stage of commitment. In the case of *In re Lee*,[10] the voluntary commitment statute was challenged on due process and equal protection grounds. The court construed the statute to permit the minor patient to seek and obtain his own release without parental consent.

In the case of *Melville v. Sabbatino*,[11] initial steps were taken to erase the distinction between voluntary and involuntary commitments. In this case the court held that the commitment of unemancipated minors by parents would be subject to the due process requirements of *In re Gault*.[12] In Tennessee, the statute permitting voluntary commitment of mentally retarded children by their parents was struck down because of the possible conflicts between parents and mentally retarded. The court felt that the juvenile procedures violated the due process clause.[13]

The case that holds the most promise for the minor is the case of *Kremens v. Bartley*.[14] In the fall of 1972 a 15-year-old boy at a Pennsylvania state hospital contacted a legal intern for advice and possible representation. The patient had been in the hospital for 10 months, having been committed by his mother. The three-judge federal court that heard the case decided that children are entitled to substantial protection against abuses in the commitment process, and dictated that a child who is being committed is entitled to certain rights: advance notice, counsel, hearings, the right to be present, the right to confront and cross-examine witnesses and to present a defense. The court recognized that taking part in an adversary hearing might be difficult for a child, but declared that this trauma "pales beside the specter of the trauma inflicted on a child erroneously committed."

The court refused to make an exception to the traditional guarantees of due process and pointed out that the child

> ... is involuntarily removed from his home and familiar surroundings and is committed to an institution where he suddenly faces the regimented routine of ward life and daily confrontations with state employees, rather than family and friends.

The court noted:

> The stigma associated with mental institutionalization may render civil commitment a more lasting abridgement of personal freedom than imprisonment for a crime.

The Supreme Court has only recently agreed to hear the *Bartley* case on Certarori, and the total impact of the case remains to be felt. If the position of the lower cout holds, there will no longer be a clear distinction between voluntary and involuntary commitments of minor patients.

The court has been vigorous in extending to children the procedural safeguards provided in the Bill of Rights for those accused of crimes.[15] The holdings of the cases are consistent with analysis which begins by assuming that children are entitled to full constitutional rights, and which proceeds to limit these rights only when accommodation is required to resolve a conflict with interests of parents, society, or what appears to be the child's best interests. Where there is a conflict between the parent and the child in cases involving a mentally disturbed child, the courts have moved to the side of the child insofar as seeing that due process is guaranteed and that the child maintains his independent right to counsel.

Where a parent has complained to the court against an allegedly emotionally disturbed child who is disobedient, the courts have recognized that the interests of parent and child are in potential conflict. In *Marsden v. Commonwealth*,[16] the court held that due process as interpreted in *In re Gault* required the accused child have right to counsel.

In the case of *In re Sippy*,[17] the court held that a mother could not control her daughter's legal representation nor waive her doctor-patient privileges for her. Thus, where a parent seeks to have a child committed to a mental hospital, the child may have opposing interests and to entrust the child's procedural and substantive rights to his parent would effectively abolish those rights.

It would seem that the judicial recognition of a minor's right to refuse initial commitment (and even treatment thereafter) might be based upon due process, as in the right to treatment cases,[18] and upon the developing constitutional right to privacy.[19] Unfortunately, the privacy doctrine has not been fully developed, but the Supreme Court has made clear it is essentially an individual right, and

> therefore its exercise by a parent in opposition to the wishes of the child, or the granting of a parental veto over the child's ability to exercise his right, would seem to contradict the spirit of privacy which is found in the right to refuse treatment. In the end, the key question remains still to be answered: Does the parent have a right distinctly and separately cognizable from the right of the child?[20]

III. PARENS PATRIAE

Thus far, under this general section of the minor's right to accept or reject treatment, we have been talking about the initial stage of treatment, that is the act of commitment to a mental institution. As in the case of where a minor is admitted to a medical hospital, there is very little that the minor can do in the end in refusing the admission. There is a difference though, in that, generally speaking, a minor can force an involuntary commitment by the court. Unlike a medical admission, this judicial commitment will carry a *prima facie* determination of illness — a fact that provides the institution with the necessary authorization to submit the child to treatment after his commitment. The child's right to accept or reject treatment once he has been admitted to the mental hospital has little support from the authorities. Where a question has been raised to the minor's right, it is based upon the nature of the treatment he or she is to receive—whether or not the treatments are to be intrusive in kind.

There is inherent in an adjudication that a minor should be committed under the state's *parens patriae* power the decision that he can be forced to accept the treatments found to be in his best interest; it would be incongruous if an individual who lacks capacity to make a treatment decision could frustrate the very justification for the state's action by refusing such treatments.[21] Generally the deprivations of forced treatment should be weighed in the initial court hearing for *parens patriae* commitments—the issue of whether commitment will be a net benefit to the minor.

As I have previously discussed, a fundamental interest in bodily privacy has been recognized both at common law and constitutional interpretive decisions. If we consider the application of highly intrusive psychiatric treatment, there is a serious legal possibility that such treatment may not only infringe on a constitutional right to prevent unwanted bodily intrusions by the state, but also abridge the freedom of speech guaranteed by the first amendment.[22] Intrusive treatment is generally taken to include psycho-surgery or chemotherapy where the psychotropic drugs used are administered to the patient in excessive dosages with unpredictable results. Some parties have also argued that electric shock treatments are intrusive.[23] Examples of non-intrusive treatments would be psychoanalysis, counseling with therapists, ordinary medical care, and some moderate drug therapy. The drug therapy must have predictable results and must not produce permanent change in the patient's mind, that is, the patient's mind is not unalterably damaged. There is no question that in treating severely mentally ill patients, some intrusive treatments involve great deprivations for the patient and can have permanent or drastic effects on a patient's mind. The National Institute of Health has recommended that psychosurgery on involuntary mental patients be prohibited. It should also be noted that behavioral control techniques, particularly aversive stimulation programs, can also have significant and permanent side effects. There, programs involve generally the use of negative stimuli to discourage self-destructive behavior such as head-banging by autistic children. The aversive stimulation can vary from squirting distasteful substances in the child's mouth to painful electric shock delivered whenever the child strikes her head against the wall. The side effects that can be produced include pain, increased aggressiveness, anxiety and somatic and physiological malfunctions.

Ultimately, however, with regard to minors, a constitutional analysis offers us no distinctive lines marking off a definitive group of prohibited treatments. While psychosurgery and certain chemotherapies are extremely intrusive and rather speculative as to what benefits they might offer to a minor patient, we can conceive of cases in which they can be forced on a *parens patriae* minor.

If a minor is so severely handicapped that no other form of treatment is available, a slim chance of benefit might outweigh the deprivations. For example, the extremely hyper-kinetic autistic child who must be constantly isolated and protected from violent activities to himself and others, might conceivably benefit from intrusive therapy. This therapy, though speculative, could affect the hyperkinetic feature of the illness and bring about some degree of stability in the child's life. There is a constitutional basis for even highly intrusive forced treatments.

Most current statutes which regulate intrusive treatments require that consent be given both by a patient where he or she is able to do so and by his or her guardian and advocate.[24]

The legal problem here is that under the standards for *parens patriae* commitments, the court would have already made the determination that the patient lacks the capacity to make treatment decisions—particularly in the case of a minor. This determination by the court would seem to negate the necessity of obtaining a consent from the patient at a later date for treatments.

Generally, however, consent is to be given by the patient, unless he is recognized as being incompetent, then proxy consent by relatives, guardian, or a court will suffice.[25]

It might be pointed out that under the New York and North Carolina laws,[26] a refusal to give consent by minor (competent or not) to intrusive treatment is uncontestable.

There are some jurisdictions, however, which authorize the superintendent of the mental hospital to override a competent minor or guardian's refusal to accept treatment. Because such refusal places a constraint on medical discretion, in California, the superintendent need only have 'good cause' while in Massachusetts, the minor's refusal can be overridden if the superintendent has good cause and obtains the consent of patient's guardian or parent.[27] In Idaho, the superintendent can merely file a petition with the court indicating the reasons why the patient's right to refuse treatment is being denied.[28]

Thus, in the final analysis, the minor has very little recourse in stopping an unwanted treatment, regardless of its nature or its intensity.

IV. JUVENILE COURT COMMITMENTS

A sharp distinction must be drawn between a *parens patriae* commitment, which is *prima facie* for the benefit of the individual and a police power commitment such as juvenile court, which *prima facie* serves in protecting public safety and the sanctity of the family. Because there is generally a finding of diminished capacity to conform to expected behavioral criteria and the law, a juvenile court commitment requires no determination of incapacity to make a treatment decision. This determination is critical in attempting to compel a patient to accept treatment. Forced treatment in such a case would violate the equal protection clause of the Constitution. In most cases if an individual were committed under police power, his or her consent would presumably be sufficient to authorize treatment or to reject the treatment. We might compare a police power commitment with criminal sentence, in that a prisoner cannot be compelled to accept treatment without his consent. A minor under these circumstances may not be compelled to accept treatment. The problem here is that the law sanctions the hospital's coercion of the minor to accept treatment, in refusing to keep a minor in the hospital unless he accepts treatment. Often the minor prefers the hospital environment to being transferred to prison or some other correctional institute. Thus, right to refuse is effectively denied.

V. INFORMED CONSENT

In my dissussion of informed consent in Chapter 3, I pointed out that where the consent issue is involved in treating physical illnesses, the minor patient faces a 'diminished capacity' chronologically imposed upon him. This issue can be compounded in the case of the minor mental patient where he faces during an involuntary commitment hearing, a judicial determination that he has no capacity to consent. Thus, the patient is often ignored and a surrogate informed consent is obtained for the minor's treatment.

The law is fairly clear on its requirements for a legally effective consent by a minor. In the case of *Cooper v. Roberts*,[29] the court said that, for there to be such a consent, the minor who agrees to invasions of his body must have or reasonably appear to have, knowledge of the actual nature of the proposed invasion. The constitutional interest in bodily privacy implies that more stringent protection of mental patients should be afforded by allowing the patient to weigh all the material information regarding a proposed medical procedure. The court cites *Canterbury v. Spence*,[30] and its holding that for a patient to be fully informed, he or she should be made aware of the risks of particular types of harm, alternative treatments, and prognosis for recovery without treatment.

What is unclear is a determination of the minor patient's capacity to consent. The case law regarding a mental patient's capacity to consent is ambiguous, and decisions support almost any position.[31] Most states recognize the minor's *prima facie* right to informed consent without the acceptance of the minor's capacity to comprehend the nature of the proposed medical procedure. In the case of the minor, the act and function of 'informing' fulfills the statutory requirement of informed consent, since the actual consent to treatment is reserved by law to the parent and the state. One exception should be noted. If the proposed treatment falls into the category of therapeutic experimentation, some states have followed Federal guidelines and require the informed consent of both the minor patient and his parent.

Obviously, in the extreme cases of mental illness, such as the profoundly retarded, autism, or catatonic schizophrenia, informed consent, or any type of consent, is impossible. This fact is recognized by the law, and thus the minor's objections must be registered by his or her parent or guardian. Though procedure of obtaining consent is not always followed by the treating medical staff, there is a legal presumption at least, that no intrusive treatments will be undertaken without such consent. For the most part, with patients of this kind, ordinary treatment is covered under the law by the original consent given at the time of admission of the patient, and/or by the committing court. From a legal standpoint, much needs to be done to clear up the existing ambiguous state of informed consent and the mental patient.

VI. THE RIGHT TO TREATMENT AFTER COMMITMENT

Thus far we have discussed the basic right of the minor mental patient to accept or refuse his commitment to a hospital and the treatment that follows. This right has only been dimly interpreted by the courts. The law, however, is extremely clear and definite on the basic right of a patient, whether adult or minor, to treatment after being admitted to the mental hospital. Once a patient has been committed to a hospital, either voluntarily or involuntarily, he cannot be relegated immediately to a custodial status; regardless of his diagnosis, he must be treated, or at least an attempt must be made to treat him. He cannot simply be ignored.

The phrase 'right to treatment' has become prominent in recent years and means more than simply the right to be admitted to a mental hospital for treatment. The courts have asserted that when the reason for committing an individual to an institution is his need for treatment, treatment must be provided for him while he is *in* treatment. The 'right to treatment' while *in* treatment, describes the obligation of the state to particular kinds of treatment for persons committed for the purpose of care and treatment such as: juvenile delinquency, retarded children, sexual psychopaths, narcotic addicts, etc.[32]

Thus, if a patient has been admitted to a mental hospital, he or she is *in* treatment, and as such has a right to a particular kind and quality of treatment. We can turn to an extreme example of this principle. For instance, despite the fact that an individual might be highly dangerous, if he is being held merely because of his incompetence to stand trial, he must either be treated, civilly committed (where he must be treated) or released.[33]

The landmark case which sets the criteria for treatment, its quality and kind, while a patient is *in* treatment, is *Wyatt v. Stickney*.[34] This was the first case to hold that the failure to provide adequate treatment to a mental patient is a violation of due process. The case was a class action brought on behalf of patients at three Alabama institutions for mentally disabled and mentally retarded patients. The plaintiff, Wyatt, claiming that the treatment they were receiving was constitutionally inadequate, sought a declaration of standards for adequate treatment while *in* treatment, as a constitutional right. The court said:

> To deprive any person of his or her liberty upon the altruistic theory that the confinement is for humane therapeutic reasons and then fail to provide adequate treatment violates the very fundamentals of due process.[35]

The rationale of this case was reaffirmed in the case of *Donaldson v. O'Conner*,[36] where the court held that the plaintiff-patient could collect damages from two state psychiatrists who had intentionally denied treatment to him. The court said:

> The rationale for confinement is the *"parens patriae"* rationale that the patient is in need of treatment, due process requires that minimally adequate treatment be in fact provided.[37]

The court also applied the same rationale to police power commitments.

The theory behind the due process analysis is that legislative means must be rationally related to legislative ends; this is to say that they must have a real and substantial relation to legislative ends. For example, we can look at *Eisenstadt v. Baird*,[38] where the court demonstrated that the ban on contraceptives was not rationally related to the valid purposes of deterring premarital sexual intercourse or protecting public health.

It should be pointed out that the right to treatment does not require that the treatment be effective; but only that such treatment be given as provides each patient a 'realistic opportunity to be cured or to improve his or her mental conditon.'[39] Under this language, a profoundly retarded minor has the right to some form of treatment that goes beyond mere custodial care; some effort is necessary by the hospital to improve his condition.

In the *Wyatt* case the court determined that there are three general institutional conditions that make up the criteria for adequate and effective individual therapy.

(1) A humane psychological and physical environment, (2) a qualified staff in numbers sufficient to administer adequate treatment, and (3) an individualized treatment plan.[40]

The court found that humane conditions had to exist for hospitalization to be truly therapeutic. These conditions were set out in the court's comprehensive order which directed the hospital to recognize *patient's rights* of enjoying privacy and dignity, being free from physical restraints and isolation unless necessitated by emergency, to wear their own clothes, keep personal possessions, to participate in religious worship, and have suitable opportunities for social contact. In addition, the patient has the right to minimum amounts of floor space and maximum ratio of patients to lavatory facilities. The court also set specific ratios not only for psychiatrists, doctors, nurses, psychologists and aides, but for stenographers and typists of records and maintenance repairmen.[41]

Last, and perhaps the most important, the individual treatment plans require an institution to focus its attention more precisely upon patients as individuals, rather than to rely on the commonly articulated theory that the mere presence of the patient in the therapeutic environment of a mental hospital constitutes 'milieu therapy.' The court order requires extensive records to be kept of each patient and include chief complaints of the patient, a copy of the individual treatment plan, a medication history, a summary of each significant patient-professional contact, and a detailed weekly summary of the patient's progress. Thus, through a far-reaching 'legislative' decision by the court, a patient in a mental hospital has a right to treatment upon his commitment to the hospital, and the right that this treatment be adequate and effective insofar as it relates to him. All this also applies to minors.

VII. RIGHT NOT TO BE PUNISHED

I have separated this right for a brief discussion from the right to treatment, even though it might be considered a part of humane treatment because the courts have recognized it clearly in some recent decisions. Because of the *Wyatt* case, a minor has the right not to be restrained except where he threatens harm to himself or to others. The rationale is because arbitrary restraints are likely to infringe fundamental interests of freedom of movement or bodily privacy, and they must be the least restrictive alternative available.

The courts recognize that within a mental institution, deprivations of liberty may be necessary to protect patients from self-inflicted injury to others. It is the institution's obligation to preserve order and to provide for the right of institutionalized persons to protection from harm. This is especially true in the case of young patients—female and male. They are particularly vulnerable to sexual assaults. The courts have extended the rationale that prisoners and other individuals confined by the state are constitutionally entitled to reasonable protection from assaults of fellow inmates.[42] Though a minor can be restrained for reasons given, the court in the *Wyatt* case made it clear that certain restrictive procedures must be followed. The patient while in restraint or isolation for punishment must be checked hourly by qualified attendants, must have hourly bathroom privileges, and must be bathed twice daily. In no case is corporal punishment permitted.[43]

VIII. INSTITUTIONAL LABOR

Recently the use of institutional labor has been challenged in the courts on two grounds: (1) A violation of the 13th amendment's ban on involuntary servitude and (2) institutional labor must be compensated according to provisions of Fair Labor Standards Act.[44] The critical question involving a minor is whether the labor was voluntarily performed. It is recognized that at times institutional pressures combine to create an atmosphere of coercion which may compel a minor to accept work assignments specific to minors against his will. For example, the minor might desire to please the therapist for an early release from the hospital. These pressures render a minor's labor involuntary within the meaning of the thirteenth amendment.[45] There is an exception to institutionalized labor though. If it can be adequately demonstrated that the consent of the minor is voluntary and that he or she has the capacity to understand the nature of the consent and is over 14 years of age, certain labor is permitted.

The court in *Jobson v. Hume*[46] recognized a difficult problem in permitting and denying institutionalized labor, in that certain kinds of labor are also legitimate forms of psychiatric treatment. This is especially true of children in treatment for drug addiction and juvenile delinquency. This case noted that civilly committed patients can be forced to accept many forms of treatment and found it difficult to distinguish work therapy from any other type of treatment in this respect. Thus, if certain types of labor are, in fact, beneficial to the minor, it would be permissible for a court to authorize such therapy and for the institution to coerce such labor. The controlling issue involved here, which I will discuss more thoroughly in my section on ethics, is the obvious lack of a minor's right to consent to his or her particular therapy.

In conclusion here, the *Wyatt* case does place a stringent condition on forced labor in holding that while labor can be compelled if it were part of the patient's individual treatment plan, the labor must *not* benefit the institution. For example, while personal housekeeping could be required without compensation, maintaining the grounds of the institution cannot be.[47]

IX. CONFIDENTIALITY

Protecting the privacy of mental patients, especially the minor, as well as the confidentiality of their communications and medical records, has become a significant legal concern. The 'right of privacy' implies the right of the individual to keep some information about himself or access to his personality (i.e., as by a photograph) completely secret from others. However, the very nature of the term 'confidentiality' presupposes a disclosure immediately threatens the concept of privacy. The mere logistics of maintaining an element of privacy in a mental institution can present serious problems. The proliferation of automated methods for recording, storing, and retrieving medical records information carries the confidential information far beyond the boundaries of the original physician-patient relationship.

For the psychiatric record, much more additional information is required than that of medical record. For example, in addition to physical information, a psychiatric history is taken, and a *mental status report* is prepared for each patient admitted. Social service reports, psychological evaluations, legal papers, records of treatment including all therapeutic activities, and progress notes are needed. A final diagnosis based on nomenclature of the Diagnostic and Statistical Manual of the American Psychiatric Association must be included. And finally, the discharge summary should be a recapitulation of the course of the patient's illness and treatment during the hospital stay. It is obvious that because of the additional information needed and the larger number of parties that have access to privileged information, the concept of confidentiality has a narrow scope of applicability when viewed realistically.

In light of the problems of protecting the minor mental patient, most states have taken steps to protect some degree of privacy.[48] All but three states (Rhode Island, Texas, and Wisconsin) recognize the right of privacy in some form, while approximately two-thirds of the states have enacted physician-patient testimonial privilege statutes which extend to mental patients. The state of Massachusetts provides the most stringent protection for mental patients and besides maintaining the confidentiality of patient records, goes on to protect patients from commercial exploitation of any kind. For example, no patient shall be photographed, interviewed or exposed to public view without either his express written consent or that of his legal guardian.[49]

The minor's right to privacy is particularly vulnerable to the 'dangerous patient' doctrine. This doctrine permits exceptions to privilege statutes as they apply to physician-patient relationship. Where the psychiatrist has reason to believe a child is dangerous to himself or to the public, he can reveal such information without violating 'privileged communication.' However, from a constitutional perspective, such justification appears suspect. In the case of *In re Lifschutz*,[50] the court held that a patient's interest in keeping confidential communications from public purview was constitutionally protected. Nonetheless, most states provide for the exception to such confidentiality by clothing the breach of privacy under the guise of the 'dangerous patient.'

Once the 'dangerous patient' exception has been invoked, then the patient's medical record becomes public property and is available for public inspection. Legally, for a child with dangerous propensities, there are only two choices for avoiding infringement of privacy, either by not discussing the matter with his therapists, or by not resisting commitment to the hospital.

The minor's right to privacy is further compromised by his lack of capacity to enter into a binding legal contract. This point was discussed in the chapter on physical illness. It is even more apparent in the context of mental illness. Both the parent and the state form a triad with the minor in his relationship to the psychiatrist. If financially solvent, the parent is responsible for professional charges as well as care and support of the minor in the institution. It makes no difference whether the child is in a private or state hospital. This responsibility entitles the parent to legal access to his child's records. In the case of public support in a state institution, the state under *parens patriae*, or juvenile court commitment, is a party to the minor's record along with the parents. The effect of this triad is to cast the psychiatrists into a dual role, a role that raises serious ethical questions which I will discuss in depth in the following section on ethics.

I will conclude this section with the observation that while the minor's right to privacy is protected for the most part by statutes, by the very nature of the illness and its place in our society, the protection afforded is extremely limited.

CHAPTER 6

MENTAL ILLNESSES — ETHICAL RIGHTS

Generally speaking, the ethical rights of children in treatment for mental illnesses are similar to those possessed by children in treatment for catastrophic illnesses. They are, however, much more complex and are difficult to unpack and analyze for discussion. It is hard to focus on 'consent rights,' the right to confidentiality, and others when considered alongside present legal rights, and the socio-legal structure for dealing with the mentally ill. Additional factors which were absent in the case of catastrophic illnesses now come into play and must be dealt with. Some of these factors which suggest the difficulty alluded to of unraveling the minor's rights are: (1) substitution of a custodial institution (sometimes referred to as a hospital, sometimes not) for a medical hospital; (2) judicially imposed commitment to a mental hospital; (3) a legally determined state of incompetency and loss of rationality—a procedure that erroneously denotes actual loss of rationality. My discussion then of the ethical rights of children in treatment for mental illnesses will be built around these factors. As in the study of catastrophic illnesses, particular emphasis will be placed on 'consent rights' and the principle of identical rights, since 'consent rights' in effect control what is to happen to the patient and all other rights (i.e., confidentiality, right to counsel, etc.) flow from the initial act of consent.

I. 'CONSENT RIGHTS'

The right of informed consent, of consent to treatment, and to refuse

79

treatment are, of course, as important ethically to the mental patient as to the hospital patient. They are not altered by the nature of an illness. Whether one is 'physically' ill or 'mentally' ill does not change the substance of these rights within the principle of equal respect and concern. However, as legal rights they are changed by the 'myth' of mental illness which surrounds the socio-legal structure and suggests to it that the rights of mental patients are different from those of medical patients. We see this difference manifested in the absence of any legal mechanism for the court commitment of a patient to a medical hospital for treatment and in the diminished role the state plays in asserting its compelling interest in seeing the medical patient treated. We also see the difference in the fact that a competent medical patient cannot be legally detained against his will in the hospital and in the patient's right to discharge at any time by his attending physician. There is also a protective element in mental health laws that does not exist in regard to the physically sick patient.

Because society's idea of a medical hospital is vastly different from that of a mental hospital, the rights associated with the two concepts are thought to be different. Ultimately, the public's concept of the indefinable term 'mental illness' formulates the basis for a difference which should not exist between the ethical and legal rights afforded to the mental patient and to the medical patient.

In recent years the term 'mental illness' has undergone all sorts of fruitless definitional exercises in an attempt to arrive at some consensus of understanding as to what it means to say a person is mentally ill. I do not intend to enter the debate here except to note that there is still a prevailing uncertainty as to the cause, diagnosis, classification and treatment of mental illness.[1] There is not, however, a lack of uncertainty as to the meaning of mental illness in the public's and law's viewpoints. There is, however, a misunderstanding of the concept (i.e., that mental illness means 'total mental incompetency' and that mentally ill patients should be institutionalized) and this misunderstanding encroaches upon the autonomous 'consent rights' being defended here within the ethical principle of equal respect and concern.

Before proceeding too far it might be noted that there is some moral support for present laws on consent; however, such support is far too narrow when viewed from the principle of identical rights as made applicable through the concept of equal respect and concern. This principle does not mean that all mental patients, adult and minors, should be treated alike, instead, all patients, medical and mental, are equally unique and should be treated as such. The mental patient possesses uniquely his own presumption of rationality just as do the medical patient and the non-patient. It can be argued that both the adult and minor mental patient may be rational in the relevant sense. This is to say that both the adult and minor patient can possess interests that are coherently ordered

80

and conduct that demonstrates a sense of deeper understanding of their own ends and values. As in the case of physical illnesses discussed in Chapter 4, if the presumption of rationality cannot be overridden, the principle of identical rights applies. However, it should be noted that the adult mental patient does *not*, in current practice, have the same legal rights as adult medical patients as enumerated in Chapter 3, and hence, cannot be used as the standard for the minor. For example, the adult medical patient can ordinarily refuse to be admitted to a medical hospital for treatment while the mental patient can be involuntarily committed to treatment. Thus, 'identical rights' for children does not mean those rights normally accorded the adult mental patient, but instead the concept embraces the totality of the legal and moral rights expressed in the doctrine of informed consent—that a rational adult has a right to determine what shall be done with his or her own body and mind.[2]

It is the involuntary court commitment that most emphatically violates the principle of equal respect and concern and sets the stage for much of the misunderstanding of the mental patient. At this time the court in its deliberations basically determines the legal competency of the minor and his need to be institutionalized for treatment. The public generally erroneously accepts that a court commitment is indicative of a diminished capacity and loss of rationality. Such a conclusion is valid for only a small portion of the cases. Certainly in those cases where it has been clearly demonstrated that the minor's emotional make-up is such that he is without question dangerous to others or himself, it might be validly argued that there is a loss of rationality which justifies paternalistic intervention. In such cases the minor cannot demonstrate any conscious ordering of the constituent elements of his end, and there is no longer any coherence and consistency between his ends and his attitude, emotions, and relations. In contrast a rational person would focus on the necessary interrelation and interaction between these elements and certainly attempt to act so as not to be dangerous to others.

The same can be argued to be true in those situations involving profoundly retarded and autistic children. There is obviously a corresponding relation between competency and rationality.

There are, however, many cases where a court commitment does not mean loss of rationality especially those dealing with the 'dangerous patient.' There is a propensity of psychiatrists to overpredict dangerousness and the tendency of the profession to become identified with the goals of law enforcement. Numerous reports confirm that psychiatrists are prone to overpredict dangerousness. In a study in New York 121 persons who had been previously adjudged 'dangerously insane' were released pursuant to a court order after it had been determined that the procedure under which they had been committed was constitutionally defective. A follow-up study on their release revealed that in the four years following the release, the group of 121 accounted for only 16 criminal convictions involving no more than nine individuals. The report concluded that the rate of conviction was not appreciably higher than that expected in a random sample of normal persons. The 16 convictions included seven for public drunkenness, four for possessing hypodermic instruments, and one each for vagrancy, petty larceny and armed robbery. In another study of 967 patients affected by the court action mentioned above, only 2.7 had been returned to the hospital for the dangerously insane.[3] There are a number of explanations possible for the reported overprediction. Some believe that psychiatrists internalize community sentiment that commitment is desirable and expected. There is a tendency of psychiatrists to second guess public desires and depend upon the public and legislative support for psychiatrists' naming certain persons dangerous in order to impose involuntary restrictions upon them.

Another equally threatening factor is the congruent roles of the psychotherapist and police officer. Psychotherapists are expected to be aware of any indications of developing danger and to take appropriate action, even to the denial of due process for the detained individual who is estopped from participating in his own defense. These same dangers are present for the patient who is committed under emergency provisions. It is not at all unusual for an emergency commitment to be transmuted into a regular involuntary commitment, especially since the presumption of the loss of rationality may continue.[4] Once a person exhibits some symptoms of illness, he is usually considered sick until proven healthy, a subtle shift in the burden of proof.

What is being argued here is that the principle of equal respect and concern requires that in every court commitment case (as well as voluntary commitments) the presumption of the patient's rationality be put at issue. This is to say that adequate inquiry should be made not only as to the emotional condition of the patient (i.e., whether dangerous or suicidal, etc.) but to the extent the presumption of rationality has been diminished or overcome. Since competent persons afflicted with physical illnesses may refuse treatment, a denial of the same right to the mentally ill who are not deemed irrational would violate the thesis of identical rights. Mental autonomy, like bodily autonomy, cannot be interfered with by the state or anyone else without first defeating the presumption of rationality.

When it has been determined that a diminished rationality exists as distinguished from a complete loss of rationality (e.g., the very young, profoundly retarded, etc.) paternalistic intervention is ethically justified only to the extent of the relationship of the diminished rationality to full rationality. This statement might at first appear to be contrary to what I have argued in Chapter 4 on catastrophic illnesses. There I spoke of a loss of the presumption of rationality; and here I am speaking of diminished rationality. It is not a shift in moral principles though. What must be kept in mind is the general distinction between treatment procedures for minor mental patients and a child suffering from a catastrophic illness. In the latter case there is generally the one major decision to be made and it is this decision that invokes a challenge to 'consent rights' of the minor—for example, the decision to amputate a leg, to refuse blood transfusions, or to remove the respirator. While this is a general difference between decision-making in catastrophic and mental illnesses, there are, however, exceptions. For instance, in the case where a patient makes the decision to undergo chemotherapy treatments for cancer, each treatment period can be considered as independent from another, in that the patient before undergoing any one treatment can decide to discontinue it.

In the former case involving the minor mental patient (outside of the areas already mentioned, i.e., the very young, profoundly retarded, etc), there is not, in most cases, just one major decision to be made but a definitive course of treatment that takes place over weeks, perhaps months and years. (An exception to this would be the decision for psychosurgery or one course of intensive chemotherapy.)

The initial act of determining a need for institutionalization, though based upon an absence of rationality, should not carry with it in every case a finding that rationality is permanently lost. To do so would allow the mental autonomy of the minor to be continuously violated without his consent. This position can best be demonstrated by looking at the following case involving a 13-year-old girl.

Cynthia K. is a 13-year-old girl, fully developed, with average intelligence. Her mother and father are divorced and Cynthia lives with her mother. Her mother suffers from paranoia and has been institutionalized on two occasions. Cynthia does not attend school regularly, and that when she does she experiences difficulty in relating to the other students and to her teachers. Her social life is rather limited, and she is extremely sexually permissive. Cynthia experiences deep guilt feelings over her 'loose morals' and often goes into deep states of depression 'after having been laid.' There have been times though when Cynthia was anxious to attend school to 'put her house in order.' During these times she is extremely diligent in her work and expresses the desire to go to college and become a nurse. She wants to marry a farmer, have three children, and live in the country.

During two occasions of deep depression, Cynthia attempted to kill herself by overdose of aspirin. After the last attempt at suicide, the state intervened *(parens patriae)* when the mother would not admit her to a mental hospital, and obtained a court order committing Cynthia to a mental institute for treatment of her depression. It should be noted that the court hearing took place while Cynthia was still deeply depressed and was completed in 20 minutes. At the hearing the court determined, based on testimony of psychiatrists, that Cynthia was a 'dangerous person' and 'dangerous to herself.'

After Cynthia's admission to the hospital, she underwent an initial course of psychotropic treatment and demonstrated remarkable improvement. She immediately expressed the desire to go home "that her Mother needed her" and she wanted to return to school. Cynthia's psychologist felt that even though she "seems to be on top of things," she should receive controlled therapy in an institutional setting for a period of at least six months. In addition to detaining Cynthia for further treatment, her freedom of movement within the institution was drastically reduced to her sleeping quarters and certain areas of the grounds because of her desire to go home.[5] The conclusion in Cynthia's case is that because Cynthia was involuntarily committed to the hospital by the court, most of her 'consent rights' had been abrogated—she could not refuse additional therapy and could be lawfully restricted to a particular area of the hospital. She certainly could not go home. Some central issues can be drawn from this case for discussion which will help us to focus on the question of minor's consent rights. (1) The initial inquiry of the committing court could have overridden the presumption of rationality, as is necessary to valid intervention. (2) It is questionable whether there is always a permanent abridgement of a presumption of rationality. (3) Any intrusion on autonomy must relate to the patient's diminished rationality (if such exists).

(1) To begin with, it is possible that the court at Cynthia's commitment hearing could have established an absence of rationality in her case (though it would have taken a more extensive procedure than she was actually granted). This is not always the case though. Just the act of attempted suicide by itself is insufficient to indicate the loss of one's rationality. While a suicidal act is thought to be generally irrational, it can be a rational decision under certain circumstances (e.g., a patient suffering from excruciating pain of terminal cancer).

It is important to point out again that under the principle of equal respect and concern, Cynthia is possessed with all of those rights previously enumerated in Chapter 4 and additional ones which I will discuss later in this chapter. Her case falls within the thesis of 'identical rights.' Under this thesis, the court should determine not only that the minor's mental condition is such that she needs treatment or that she needs treatment to protect her own welfare, but (as an additional step) because of her condition, the presumption of her rationality has been overcome with resulting diminished or lost capacity. The 'law' and 'ethics' take different roads here, and much of this difference is based on my earlier point—the misunderstanding of mental illness.

In its inquiry, the court is concerned with the need for treatment—what is best for the child from a legal viewpoint, and this determination carries with it, an accompanying assumption (which might be true or false)

84

of the loss of rationality and capacity. The child's consent rights are largely ignored and the inequitable burden is placed on the minor of defending the presumption of her rationality. If every mental illness automatically rendered the affected individual incapable of rational decision-making regarding the advisability of hospitalization, there would be no due process objection of any ethical objection to *parens patriae* commitments based solely on the presence of mental illness. However, psychiatric literature indicates that many forms of mental illness have a highly specific impact on their victims, leaving decision-making capacity and reasoning ability otherwise largely unimpaired.[6] In other areas of the law, the loss of capacity to undertake the relevant function rather than the mere presence of a mental illness is required to justify invoking *parens patriae* commitments. For example, in the area of contracts, a showing that the individual is mentally ill, or suffers from delusions, is not sufficient to establish that the person lacks the requisite capacity. In the case of *Kelly v. Davis*,[7] the defendant through his guardian sought to have a trust deed which he had executed voided, thereby negating a foreclosure on the trust deed. The facts of this case are particularly interesting in that they demonstrate how far the court is willing to go to maintain competency in business transactions. The court's focus is always on a particular act rather than a general incompetency. The defendant had been a patient at a Veteran's Administration hospital with the diagnosis of dementia praecox (schizophrenia) mixed type. He was discharged against medical advice; however, no guardian was appointed for him at the time. The psychiatrist testified that he had examined the defendant on three separate occasions over a period of one and a half years and in his opinion the defendant was incompetent. Many members of the defendant's family along with friends also testified that the defendant was incompetent.

The plaintiff's proof consisted of numerous lay witnesses testifying that they had transacted business with the defendant and that the defendant always seemed to understand the essential elements of the business transacted. A merchant, banker, and lawyer testified that they saw nothing to indicate incompetency. The defendant had also purchased a farm, rented equipment, and testified in two law suits. The court held:

> In all cases where incapacity arising from defect of the mind is alleged, the issue is not whether the mind is itself diseased, or the person is afflicted with any particular form of insanity, but rather whether the powers of the mind have become so affected, by whatever cause, as to render him incapable of transacting business like the one in question.[8]

The distinction between forms of mental illness is also embodied in the law of gifts. In the case of *In re Stephen's Will* the testator was transferred from Sing-Sing prison to Donnemora State Hospital on the certificate of a physician that he was insane. After the testator's death in the hospital, his will was contested on the grounds that he was incompetent at the time it was executed. The court in upholding the will held that the operative fact to be proved is mental incompetency not insanity. Mere proof of mental weakness or insanity is not enough to invalidate an agreement or a will or a gift. In order to constitute mental incompetency, the mental disorder must be such as to destroy the capacity of the party to understand the questioned transaction in particular. The court held in effect that a person may be insane but yet competent in isolated transactions.[9]

It is also settled that incompetency to stand trial is not established by the fact that the defendant suffers from a mental illness. In the case of *United States v. Adams*,[10] the defendant was mentally ill and contested the right to be tried. The court ruled that mental illness alone was insufficient to justify defendant's position and that incompetency to stand trial is defined in terms of the defendant's inability "to consult with his lawyer with a reasonable degree of understanding" and his lack of a "rational as well as factual understanding of the proceedings." It should be pointed out that present commitment statutes often provide that commitment does not even raise a presumption of incapacity to manage property, to vote, to marry, to contract, or to engage in other activities. Yet the patient is denied his right to decision-making because of incapacity and *parens patriae* is exercised.[11]

What is being argued here is that mental illness alone is improper as a threshold standard for *parens patriae* commitments in light of the medical and legal recognition of the distinction between mental illness and incapacity. The principle of 'identical rights' is clearly violated unless loss of rationality and accompanying incapacity are made a necessary condition for commitments. Because of the element of rationality, the mental patient is entitled to the same rights accorded to the physically ill patient, and he is afforded the same due process and equal protective dimensions of the Constitution together with the same interpretive legal force of informed consent. This is not so if mental illness is made the sole criterion of commitment. For example, civil commitment statutes authorize different treatment of the mentally ill and the physically ill by subjecting the mentally ill to compulsory care while allowing the latter to choose whether to seek treatment. There is no state statute under which a physically ill individual can be involuntarily hospitalized solely because he needs treatment to protect his own welfare. Moreover, no court has ever ordered a *competent* adult to accept hospitalization and medical treatment solely for his own benefit.[12]

From the medical studies presented it can be plausibly argued that since a mentally ill person may be equally as capable of evaluating the desirability of obtaining medical care as is a physically ill individual, commitment laws which employ mental illness as the criterion which separates the committable from the noncommittable fail to meet the test of equal respect and concern. Since the purpose of utilizing an incapacity standard is to separate those persons (adults and children), whose decisions to refuse treatment must be accepted as final, from those whose choices may be validly overridden through *parens patriae* commitments, the standard should focus on the ability to engage in a rational decision-making process rather than on the resulting decision. In Cynthia's case this would entail an intensive study of all of the pertinent socio-medical facts of her case. The standard perfunctory examination of two medical doctors that Cynthia presents a danger to herself is not enough to dismiss the presumption of rationality. By proper questioning of the witnesses and the patient (where possible), suitable evidence can be compiled by the court for a proper determination of the extent of Cynthia's loss of rationality and her incapacity. If, for example, Cynthia remained in deep depression and was unable to participate in her own defense and to interact with the court and her attorney, it would seem proper for the court to make a *prima facie* finding of loss of rationality and to intervene on her behalf. From this point on, though, any step taken on Cynthia's behalf must be an 'acceptable' step—one that Cynthia would accept as the best thing for her if and when her rationality developed or was restored.

(2) With the exception of the obvious cases (i.e., very young, profoundly retarded, autistic child, etc.), any court finding of patient incapacity is qualified. In Cynthia's case and similar ones, it is always questionable whether the presumption of rationality has been permanently overcome, that it is permanent total incapacitation rather than a continuing degree of diminished capacity. Studies have demonstrated that patients may experience periods when their capacity to choose and understand is lessened or temporarily lost. There are many cases where the patient will manifest irrationality to certain specific situations and complete rationality to everything else.[13]

In Cynthia's case, while the presumption of her rationality may have been overridden at the court hearing, her responsive conduct and actions following the initial therapy indicated *prima facie* a return to capacity and thus re-establishment of the presumption of rationality. What I am suggesting here is that a court commitment should not be a license to permit a continuing legal assault upon any patient's consent rights. The possibility that the minor has developed or regained rationality and decision-making capacity must be entertained and confronted by the mental health professionals at each stage of the patient's treatment. What began as an ethically valid paternalistic act ceases to be valid if the patient's capacity is restored. An analogy to this situation can be found in legal discourse on the 'presumption of innocence' in criminal law. The presumption of innocence, which is perhaps the most fundamental right to be relied on in a criminal trial, can be overridden. This fact does not mean, however, that the presumption is not present in subsequent criminal inquiries or trials concerning new events. The presumption must be challenged anew in every criminal trial of an individual. Unfortunately, the presumption of rationality is not accepted with the ease and understanding that the presumption of innocence is. Rather, the uneasiness in which the public approaches mental illness (as distinguished from physical illness) is manifested in court commitments and continuing disregard for the consent rights of children.

(3) The idea of diminished rationality carries with it the presence of diminished autonomy, and any intrusion on this autonomy must relate to the patient's diminished rationality (that area of his rationality which is diminished). Thus, paternalistic actions are limited to those decision-making areas in which the presumption of rationality has been overridden. This is particularly applicable in mental cases as distinguished from most medical cases. In the medical case of the 11-year-old girl requesting termination of hemodialysis treatment,[14] her rationality is to be challenged at that particular point. It could have been challenged at the onset of her treatment if she had decided then to refuse treatment. We may assume that her mental faculties will remain the same, from the beginning of her illness until the critical time for deciding to terminate treatment, though they certainly can be affected by external factors such as pain and internal ones such as despair or hopelessness. While these factors may work as catalytic elements to influence decision-making, they do not directly alter one's rational nature as psychotropic drugs do. This is different from the critically injured patient who cries out while in excruciating pain to be mercifully killed, and who is unable to rationally grasp the total picture of his injury and ultimate recovery. It can be compared to some mental patients whose 'capacity' is only temporarily lost. We can understand this by looking at Cynthia's case again. Cynthia attempted to kill herself twice while in a state of deep depression. Such a state is constructed around a total abandonment of any hope, and a resolution to escape from what seems to be an array of insurmountable problems. It is a state of unbelievable unhappiness. There is a withdrawal from participating in the 'real' world and a disengagement from any interaction with people. As in the case of the critically injured patient, Cynthia was unable to focus on anything beyond her temporary sickness and to rationally understand her depressive state and the possibility of a recovery.

If a paternalistic intrusion on a patient's autonomy must relate to the degree and location of the patient's diminished capacity, what does this hold for children? It means simply that paternalistic intervention beyond the initial act of court commitment and treatment ordered is ethically invalid. The consent rights within the thesis of identical rights remain very much alive. At the conclusion of each particular stage or course of treatment, the extent of the patient's rationality must be examined in order to ascertain those areas, if any, where the patient's autonomy has been restored. There can be no ethically valid intrusion into those areas. These areas might be somewhat nebulous, and the nebulousness could affect the overall integrity of the patient's capacity, but they should be respected. To allow patient-autonomy in limited areas while continuing to exercise paternalistic prerogatives in the other areas of the patient's life should present no insurmountable problems. This fact certainly would allow for the deinstitutionalization of a multitude of patients, both adult and minor, who can function quite well in society with diminished capacity.

It should be noted that the three points discussed are present in all *parens patriae* court commitment cases as well as voluntary commitments and juvenile court commitments. While all of the arguments previously presented are equally applicable both in situations involving the voluntary commitment of a minor by his parent or guardian, and in the juvenile court commitment of a minor, a brief discussion of some particular issues regarding the latter is in order.

With respect to the consent rights of a minor, no ethical distinction can be made between a voluntary commitment and an involuntary one. Like its counterpart (involuntary commitment), a voluntary commitment institutionalizes the minor. The parent or guardian, acting under sanction of the law, is armed with legal authority to unilaterally commit the child to the mental institution. The commitment can be for life (e.g., profoundly retarded) or for undetermined durations. The admittance requirements are essentially the same as for an involuntary commitment; that is, necessary testimony by doctors (generally two) as to the need for treatment. Many times the voluntary commitment is changed to an involuntary commitment when the minor balks at being admitted to the hospital. As in the case of involuntary commitment, there is no determination of capacity and rationality. Court commitment does have the added weight of the proposed treatment being legally sanctioned.

One bright exception should be noted to the above statements, regarding children 16 years and older. Some state codes now provide that a 16-year-old child can voluntarily commit himself to a mental institution without parental consent. Such a law is congruent with the ethical arguments being offered here. There is one problem, however. If the 16-year-old desires to sign himself out from the mental institution and terminate treatment, his voluntary commitment can be terminated and his status altered to involuntary commitment by application of either the hospital staff or his parents. The patient can be detained for 48 hours while the application is being prepared and filed with the court and then detained indefinitely until the hearing and receipt by the hospital of either an involuntary commitment order or dismissal order. For all practical purposes this legal maneuver has the effect of making all voluntary commitments potentially involuntary ones, depending on the professional discretion of the hospital staff. It should be noted here that in most jurisdictions the 48-hour detainment procedure is applicable to adult patients as well as minor patients.

Of the three types of institutional commitments, the juvenile court commitment is the one that is most different and does not seem, at first glance, to belong here. The voluntary commitment by the parent or guardian, and the *parens patriae* involuntary commitment, are at least *prima facie* thought to be paternalistic actions motivated out of concern for the minor's interest. In those cases the patient's mental capacity can be directly involved.

A juvenile court commitment is a constitutionally sanctioned exercise of police powers; powers which are directed toward protecting primarily, the public's safety and the sanctity of the family, and only secondarily, the interest of the minor. A case of this type generally does not involve any direct concern and determination of the mental capacity or incapacity of the child, but is instead a judically determined finding that the minor does not have the capacity to conform to normative and legal behavioral criteria. I suppose one could argue, in a technical sense, that a juvenile court commitment is a form of paternalistic intervention and that in a real sense a minor's presumption of rationality is challenged. This challenge is incorporated in the court's finding of an incoherent ordering of the juvenile's goals in relation to society's. The presumption of rationality is applicable as a principle with respect to both the total goals of society and those of its individual members. Under the criteria of rationality being employed here, there is a coherent ordering of rules and principles necessary to achieve those goals. This does not mean that every individual's goals to be coherently ordered must be identical with society's. It does mean, though, that the individual's goals must demonstrate some consistency in their interaction with and their relation to the goals of others in the sense that they will not unlawfully interfere with the pursuit of those goals. It is in this vein that certain ends of society are set; namely, the establishment of moral and legal principles that will in fact provide protection for the individual's coherent ordering of his ends. Thus, the juvenile who demonstrates emotional instability to the extent that it is disruptive to society's ends might be said to have an incoherent ordering of his goals in relation to society's (for example, adolescent prostitution). This can be an opening for sophistry, however, because many children are committed by juvenile court for conduct that if performed by an adult would be quite legal and uncommittable offenses. For example, a female

90

juvenile age 12, who demonstrates sexual promiscuity can be considered delinquent by a juvenile court and committed to an institution for therapy, while an adult woman by contrast certainly cannot be committed simply because she is sexually promiscuous. There must be other extenuating circumstances that accompany her sexual promiscuity such as retardation or schizophrenia.

The adult's actions, though morally questionable by some people, are not inconsistent with society's principle of adult autonomy and the right to privacy in these matters. In the case of the young female juvenile, because her conduct is thought to be in conflict with society's goals of what is expected of children, she is committed. Thus, though questionable, in this type of case, the juvenile's goals can be said to be incoherently ordered in relation to society's.

Because a juvenile court commitment is a constitutional exercise of police powers, the consent rights of the minor are given constitutional dimensions and are fully protected at the hearing.[15] The rights which are overridden in voluntary and involuntary commitments—refusal of therapy—are generally retained by the minor for the duration of his confinement because police powers generally may not compel a patient to accept treatment. The only recourse taken by the law in the case of refusal is to remand the minor to a detention home unless he accepts treatment—a coercive action which in itself presents ethical problems.

I might point out an inconsistency which exists between the law and ethics that adds an ironic note to what has been said. Where generally the law goes far beyond what ethics will permit in encroaching on 'consent rights' of minors, the juvenile court commitment can in some instances provide just the opposite. Paternalistic intervention might be ethically justifiable where a minor is suffering from loss of rationality, yet forced treatment in such a case, if admitted by juvenile court, would violate the equal protection clause of the Constitution.

What has been discussed thus far are the central issues involved in the confrontation between consent rights of children and paternalistic commitments to treatment in a mental hospital. One must keep in mind that the commitment is only the first condition and that the two equally important conditions must be met also: (1) An attempt to identify the interests of the minor through verbal communication and other means such as behavioral observance, (2) the ultimate acceptance by him (when rational) that the decisions made on his behalf were the best thing for him at the time. Thus, in the case of the profoundly retarded child, even though communication is impossible, the decision to institutionalize the child for life rather than to maintain him at home must be one that the child would adopt retrospectively as the best course for him if he suddenly were to become rational.

There is one argument that might be raised which allows for a possible exception to the 'acceptability' condition. Conceivably, in a few types of cases, the act of intervening might restructure or change the values of the minor patient from what they would have been had there been no paternalistic intervention. Thus, how the patient views a decision made on his behalf after he develops rationality will be influenced by these values. This might be compared to the Heisenberg effect recognized in physics, where a specific external act alters the phenomena. We can use the Jehovah's Witness case as an example. Suppose that a 5-year-old Jehovah's Witness faces death unless he receives a blood transfusion and suppose the state intervenes over the objection of the boy and his parents. Even though his life is saved, the boy might be rejected by his parents and church to the extent that he is no longer a Jehovah's Witness. In such a case, the boy's values might be altered from those that he would have had and wanted to have had, and after his rationality has developed, he might very well reject the decision made on his behalf. Such a situation, where religious preferences are involved, clouds ethical solutions and underscores the need to focus on the second condition—the needs, interests, and goals of the patient.

In Cynthia's case, some communication might have been possible. The decision to commit her for treatment, along with the kind of treatment, must be such that she would later accept when her rationality was restored. Would she accept interference with her attempts at suicide? Would she accept the psychotropic drugs as a method of healing her depressive states? These and other similar ethical questions must be resolved before any paternalistic act can be ethically validated.

What is obvious, then, is the immense burden placed on the paternalistic agent or agents in determining an 'acceptable decision.' As I previously indicated in Chapter 3 on catastrophic illnesses, many parents simply cannot fulfill the demands placed on the agent. This fact is even more obvious in cases of mental illness. The parent can be 'at war' with the child, or a parent be driven to institutionalize his retarded child simply to relieve severe physical and emotional stress or because he lacks family finances. For many parents, a mentally sick child is an embarrassment and simply too much to cope with. Thus, who the agent is becomes especially important in these cases as the means to reaching the right decision or the 'acceptable' decision from the child's point of view. Because this is so, other ethical rights besides consent rights become important. These rights (to be discussed now in the last section) though independent, are directly connected to paternalistic decision-making and must be treated fully within the principle of equal respect and concern.

The principle of equal respect and concern, and its expression in the thesis of identical rights, denotes the right to treatment as an equal, which is the right, not to receive the same burden or benefit, but to be treated with the same respect and concern as anyone else. The right to treatment as an equal, in cases of mental illnesses, exists both before and during the patient's commitment, as well as before and after any paternalistic intervention. To be treated with the same respect and concern as anyone else means that the rights a person has before commitment are retained after commitment. Thus, while consent rights can be abrogated under certain specific conditions, these rights are not washed away in the sense that they no longer exist. The right to treatment as an equal means that the mental patient's consent rights are not lost. They continue in a different dimension—the dimension of proxy representation. Thus, what a non-mental patient would consent to is consented to by the paternalistic agent, or guardian *ad litem*, or some other appointed official who has the responsibility to abide by the second and third conditions of valid paternalism. However, the right to treatment as an equal does not stop here. Those rights available to the nonmental adult patient must be made available to the minor before and during any commitment (i.e., right to counsel) and while he is a patient at the hospital. In most situations these rights are not honored, although in two isolated cases the minor's right to counsel has been upheld.

If we view the right to treatment as an equal as a balancing scales with the competent adult patient standing on one scale with his exercisable consent rights, then the mental patient's (minor or adult) side must be equally balanced with the weight of respect and concern. For example, in the area of decision making, this is done through meeting the condition that any decision made on behalf of the patient be ultimately 'acceptable' to him. There are other areas though which need to be examined, and which require respect and concern to insure the right to treatment as an equal.

II. DUAL LOYALTIES, PATIENT ADVOCATES, AND CONFIDENTIALITY

The first of these areas touches on the dilemmas of dual loyalties and patient advocates. Should a child have the right to his own psychologist or psychiatrist and to be represented solely? It seems we must answer in the affirmative if it is necessary to insure the minor the right to treatment as an equal. The problem of duality in the role of psychiatrist or psychologist has always been an ethical issue. One of the most extreme views of the situation is held by Thomas Szasz who concluded that in an institutional setting such as a state mental hospital, the psychologist is the involuntary patient's adversary at every point of their encounter.[16] This is probably true when taken with the Rawlsian conditions for paternalistic actions.

Under Rawls's second condition, the interests and goals of the patient must be of primary importance to the paternalistic agent and taken into consideration by him in any decision to be made for the patient. A clear-cut defense of the patient's interest is very difficult where the agent wears two coats—one in discharging his duties and obligations to the institution, and the other in fulfilling his obligations to the patient.

Even if the institutional personnel are not adversaries to the child patient, the institutional setting is the one in which there are differing interests and in which potential conflicts may arise. A lawyer cannot sit on both sides of his client's case. Thus, for example, when parents seek to have a child committed and have retained a psychiatrist to support their desire, or the state has intervened under *parens patriae*, there is a need for independent counsel and psychiatrist to represent the child. Without such a procedure, the psychiatrist, as a witness for the state or parents, is centered on the horns of an ethical dilemma by attempting to serve both traditional one-to-one doctor-patient relationships and the institution or parent for whom he works. In such cases, it is obvious that decisional powers can cause conflict. The potentiality of conflict is sufficient to negate consideration as an equal unless the minor has the unqualified right (and this means resources to exercise the right) to his own personal psychiatrist and counsel. Without this balancing of rights, it is doubtful that an "acceptable" decision can be reached.

If we look at the initial step taken at the time a legal procedure is invoked to commit the minor, we will see that the minor is at a distinct disadvantage in protecting his right to treatment as an equal. He is faced with adversaries and legal machinery which enable him to be declared mentally ill by a simple signing of papers. Since commitment to a mental hospital does involve restriction of personal freedom, the child should be told he does not have to speak to the psychiatrist employed by the state or his parents and that he is going to be examined with regard to his mental condition. (Obviously this stricture cannot apply to the voiceless patient.) And any statements he makes may be the basis for commitment. He then should be furnished with a patient's advocate who can provide the initial independent neutral proxy representation necessary for determination of the presence or absence of treatment as an equal. Meeting this condition may include the hiring of independent medical personnel and the advocate's own determination that the minor's presumption of rationality is overridden. I do not intend to establish here the mechanics for the operation of patient advocate role. The concept of such a role has already been adopted by a few states.[17] What is necessary is the recognition of the right for such proxy representation as the balancing factor called for by the principle of equal respect and concern.

I would suggest that the right to proxy representation is not limited to commitment procedures but endures for the duration of the minor's institutionalization. For example, child therapists need to recognize that they are morally bound to serve as an advocate too for child-clients and that the continuing presence of a patient advocate is the child's guarantee that they will be his advocate.

It might help us to understand the important balancing element of patient advocacy if we look briefly at the ways in which administrative responsibilities conflict with the patient's interest. This should help us to accept the right to advocacy being argued for.

Decisions which can be termed "administrative" encroach on the minor's right to equal respect and concern. For example, institutions must survive to give treatment, and one way of surviving is to have patients. In such conditions, a child can be falsely detained for more therapy until a new patient is admitted to take his place. Also, institutions desire to function smoothly, thus they try to keep physician-patient confrontations at a minimum. Here a child's interest might be neglected because they conflict to such an extent with the institution's that any confrontation with the child would be disruptive to the overall operations of the institution. Finally, an individual child may be denied special treatment because of limited resources and the need of other children for treatment.[18] In this type of case, the denial of treatment to a child might be rationalized on the basis of its therapeutic ineffectiveness; that is, the institution or its agent might agree that the treatment will be of little use to the child, or will not benefit him as much as it will others. Whether a decision is merely administrative or actually therapeutic is frequently difficult to determine. Thus, advocacy is needed in the wings where a decision can be interpreted as a need for money, or to function smoothly (good public relations) and the discharge or treatment of the child delayed.

The use of therapists in state mental institutions or in private mental hospitals brings us logically to another important dilemma—the question of confidentiality. How can therapists respect rights of the minor to privacy in these institutions?

In both the public and private institutions, the therapists as well as the rest of the professional staff, are being paid by the institution. In the case of the public the therapist has definite administrative commitments to the institution which often are impossible to reconcile with commitments to the child-patient. With the private institution, not only are there administrative commitments, there is the contractual commitment to the financially responsible party. This can be the minor's parents or insurance companies, or both.

Another critical issue in the child's right to confidentiality is the question whether parents should be allowed to have access to child's medical records. Both the issue duality-of-role and the issue of privacy are involved here. The traditional position of the psychiatric profession is that the psychiatrist is the agent of the patient and will act only on his behalf. Professional conduct includes securing the confidentiality of records. When a parent seeking to have a child committed goes to a hospital official or a private psychiatrist, the psychiatrist's position with respect to the child becomes less clear-cut. In the case of minor voluntary patients, the legal volition involved is that of the parent. While the goal of the psychiatrist may be expressed as the best interests of the child, it is the parent who has come to seek help, who seems the most reliable source of information, and who is paying the psychiatrist's fee. The psychiatrist can thus all too easily be tempted to become the agent of the parent in the parent-child confrontation. In these types of cases, that the patient advocate (with the assistance of a court if necessary) could weigh the decision to release any private records to the parent, the child or his proxy should be consulted to see how he feels about his parents or anyone else seeing the records.

As a concluding point to confidentiality, all children or their proxy representative should have access to their own records, including health services personnel's work notes. 'Work notes' are presently the center of legal and ethical debates relating to release of records. The argument being that work notes are really the work-property generated by the efforts of the medical person and as such are the property of that person. They are for his own use and could be deemed on occasions to be anti-therapeutic to the patient. It is my position that work notes are often the 'real' medical record and that the institutional record is only technical in its contents. Where the child is involved, his advocate should be permitted to view all of the records, 'work notes' and technical, and decide along with the medical personnel the advantages and disadvantages of making the record available to the child.

III. LABELLING AND FAMILY THERAPY

There are two rights which the right to treatment as an equal suggests but which have no legal outlet at this time. The first involves labelling, viz., the right not to be labeled 'crazy' or 'mentally ill.' The label of 'mentally ill' is almost irrevocably attached to a person through his hospitalization. In his studies, Thomas Scheff argues that the 'crazy' label can have a powerful impact upon the self-concept of the person institutionalized. He suggests that this is the single most important cause of 'careers of residual deviance.'[19] Where eccentric behavior was tolerated in normal persons, similar behavior in a former child patient will be seen as evidence of continued mental illness. Although the child is healthy mentally, the child's illness will be re-established in his actions causing a confirmation of the 'crazy' label. The label will be renewed over and over again by the public. If a minor no longer exhibits any symptoms of mental illness, he is not considered to be well but only in a period of 'remission.' There is the implication in the 'remission label' that at some future time the minor will begin to behave in a mentally sick manner again.

The child's right not to be labelled is an extension of his right to be treated as an equal. There should be the necessary protective machinery to erase the threat of labelling.

For example, the labelling and singling out of hospitals as 'mental' or 'psychiatric' institutions should be avoided. All references to a hospital as a 'mental' hospital could be dropped by legislative act. References to specific forms of 'mental illness' such as schizophrenia could also be terminated. This last step alone would go a long way toward alleviating much of the public's concern with mental patients. Also court commitments could be conducted with a greater measure of privacy, similar to adoption hearings where the real name of the child is not used or mentioned. Many other steps along the lines mentioned can be taken to assure the minor of his place in society.

The second right deals with the minor's treatment and his family. Whatever the cause of the minor's illness, the difficulties of the child often cannot be differentiated from disorders within the family. This was demonstrated in the case involving Cynthia.[20] In the case of voluntary and involuntary commitments, the law distorts the choice between family integrity and personal autonomy, for it seems to base its choice on the perception of the family situation held by one part of the family, the child's parents.[21] Laing writes that "we can never assume that the people in the situation know what the situation is."[22] The law seems to hold that there is a conclusive presumption that the parent's perception is correct. However, if the child in a family is disturbed, the parents may be the disturbing agents.

In a prehospitalization study, it was shown that in 25% of the complaints of alleged mental illness of minors, the complaintant, rather than the prospective patient evidenced signs of mental illness. From this study and others, the conclusion emerges that children suffer in many cases in the role of 'scapegoat' for the family. In the instances of scapegoating through a child, the isolated treatment of the child will not solve the child's problem; the pressures to act deviantly will continue with any family contact. The focus of therapy must then be on the family situation. The right to commit the child in these and similar types of situations must not therefore be unilateral. The child has a corresponding right to require the parents to undergo therapy with him. Anything less would negate the principle of equal respect and concern and the right to treatment as an equal.

I should like to end my essay with a few concluding comments and observations. I have shown the following:

(1) That a wide disparity exists between the legal and moral rights of children in treatment for catastrophic and mental illnesses. (I have very briefly summarized these rights below.)

(2) There is a clear and convincing line, though inequitable and unethical at times, between the legal rights of children and those of adults while in treatment for catastrophic and mental illnesses.

(3) The differences between a physically ill patient and a mental

patient are not as great as have been generally supposed.

The rights under (1) and (2) can be summarized as follows:

a. A minor between the ages of 0-16 years has the very narrow (almost absent) legal right to consent to and refuse treatment for physical and mental illnesses. The minor possesses this right morally, unless paternalistic intervention is justified on his behalf. Generally, a competent adult can be said to possess both the legal and moral right to consent to and refuse medical treatment as a part of the doctrine of informed consent.

b. A minor has only limited protection to confidentiality. The protection provided for him is statutory and applies to the most private matters of abortion, birth control, and treatment for veneral diseases. There is little, if any, right to confidentiality for the minor mental patient. The minor possesses the same moral right to privacy as the adult. There is one exception, proper paternalistic intervention would allow the inclusion of the paternalistic agent in matters of confidence and a determination of others to be brought into the privacy of the minor.

c. The minor has the legal and moral right to counsel in all involuntary commitment hearings. Though he has the moral right, he does not at this time have a legal right to counsel at voluntary commitments. There is no difference in adult rights here.

d. The minor does not have a clear legal right to counsel when being admitted to a medical hospital though he certainly possesses a moral right to one.

e. The minor has the moral right to a patient's advocate at any stage of his institutionalization in either a mental hospital or medical hospital. At this time, only a limited number of states provide for the presence of a patient advocate in mental hospitals.

I have suggested that Rawls and Dworkin furnish the ethical framework to support some existing legal rights possessed by children, and that this framework supports certain moral rights which should be legal rights. I have also argued that their concept of justice as equal concern and respect allows for the principle of 'identical rights.' This principle dictates that the rights of the minor should be identical to those of the adult while *in* treatment for catastrophic and mental illnesses unless a paternalistic intervention can be ethically validated. The three necessary conditions for validating a paternalistic intervention with the identical rights of the minor are:

(1) The principle of the presumption of rationality that applies to all persons must be overridden.

(2) The interests, goals, and values of the minor must be determined, insofar as possible, through verbal communication with the child, behavioral observance, etc., and made the basis of the decision.

(3) The decision made on behalf of the minor must be acceptable to him, when his rationality develops or is regained, as being the best thing for him at the time.

My study of children in treatment for catastrophic and mental illness has focused on existing legal rights and ethical rights in the abstract. Any serious application of the principle of identical rights would be confronted at different times with competing circumstances and values, which in the end, would have to be weighed by the courts in determining the prevailing value. Without a doubt, these hard cases would come along. It is not my intention to attempt here any resolution of the conflicting values; however, they should be recognized for what they are and a few words said about them.

The family concept occupies a special position in our society. From an ethical viewpoint, the family unit establishes special obligations, such as care and trust, values which are unique to the relationship. Historically, the law has imposed similar obligations and restraints on the family because of the family's importance to the structure and stability of society. For example, a sacred principle of common law holds that the husband and wife cannot sue each other in tort, nor can a child sue his parents in tort. To do so, the law says, would be to undermine the integrity of the family unit and is against public policy. Thus, the conflicting values of family integrity versus the rational minor's right to consent to and refuse medical treatment could provide the hard case. Will the family be destroyed in the case where a dying child refuses medical treatment against the wishes of his parents? Or perhaps more importantly, would such a situation establish a precedent that might be argued analagously in other court cases involving confrontations between parent and child? These thought provoking questions go to the very core of the issue of self-determination versus the family. From the adult's viewpoint, the doctrine of parental authority would seem to be squarely on line, its survival at stake. However, it has been there before and has survived in some instances, and been dismissed in others by the Supreme Court. (e.g., the abortion and contraceptive cases)

Another conflicting value which could raise a serious problem is the right of the child to select his own physician and/or psychiatrist. This is an adult right. Would the physician recognize a dying child as his patient to the extent that the parents would be excluded from the decision-making process? What if the physician believes that a particular dying 13-year-old child can make a rational decision to terminate all treatment or undergo radical surgery? Obviously, without a protective statute, the physician will in all probability want to side with the parents though the ethics of the situation might call for something else.

Greater problems would seem to be involved with the values of the child's right to counsel and confidentiality. To allow a minor the right to counsel would immediately place the child and his parents in the roles of adversaries. If the decision making process is reduced to the final act of a court order, the relationship of the family members will, in all probability, never be the same. However, where the parents are in fact the adversaries, a court conclusion can not be escaped, regardless of its damaging consequences. The danger of denying counsel, or the right to be represented in the decision making process might be far greater than any residual adverse consequences. This fact has been recognized by the courts in juvenile court proceedings.

The right of confidentiality would raise many issues similar to those raised by the right to counsel, and then some. Should the parent be denied access to his child's medical records where he is obligated to pay the medical bill? What if the minor does not want his parents to know anything about his illness? There is already some precedent though for denying parents access to their child's medical records. (e.g., treatment for social diseases, abortion, etc.) Nonetheless, the child's right to confidentiality would result in some hard cases down the road.

In these closing remarks, I have touched on some of the competing values that might confront the minor's right of self-determination under the principle of identical rights. There are of course many more that would have to be taken into account, such as: physician liability, patient liability, the compelling interest of the state, hospital policies, and insurance programs. However, it would seem that an earnest application of the principle of justice as equal concern and respect would alleviate many of the more stressful ethical issues arising out of the treatment of children. That the principle of identical rights would decrease significantly the disparity between a minor's legal rights and his moral rights, so that in the end a greater harmony will be brought to the community.

NOTES

Chapter 1 Introduction and General Considerations

1. *Tinker v. Des Moines School District,* 397 U.S. 503.
2. Richard Wasserstrom, "Rights, Human Rights and Racial Discrimination," *Journal of Philosophy,* Vol. 61 (1964).
3. Joel Feinberg, "The Nature and Value of Right," *The Journal of Value Inquiry,* Vol. 4 (1970), 243-257.
4. A.L. Melden, *Rights and Right Conduct* (Oxford: Basil Blackwell, 1959), pp. 18-20.

Chapter 2 The Historical Perspective of Children's Rights

1. Richard Farson, *Birthrights* (New York: Macmillan Publishing Company, 1974).
2. Philippe Aries, *Centuries of Childhood* (New York: Alfred A. Knapf, 1962).
3. Ibid.
4. Ibid.
5. Robert F. Drinin, "The Rights of Children in Modern American Family Law," in Albert E. Wilkerson, ed., *The Rights of Children: Emergent Concepts in Law and Society* (Temple University Press, 1973).
6. The prohibition against an illegitimate child inheriting from his father extends only to statutory descent and distribution. A father certainly can leave his illegitimate child property by will.
7. Richard Farson, *Birthrights.*
8. *Nan Berger, "The Child, the Law, and the State," in Paul Adams, ed., Children's Rights Toward the Liberation of the Child* (New York: Praeger Publishers, 1971).
9. Ibid.
10. Thomas Hobbes, *Leviathan* (London: J. Bohn, 1839), Molesworth ed., Vol. 3, p.257.
11. John Locke, *The Second Treatise of Government* (New York: Bobbs-Merrill, 1952), Sec. 60.
12. John Stuart Mill, *On Liberty* (New York: Washington Square Press, 1963), p. 207.
13. Ibid., p. 160.
14. Ibid., p. 207.
15. Adele D. Hofman and Harriet F. Pilpel, "The Legal Rights of Minors," *The Pediatric Clinics of North America,* 20:989, November 1973.
16. Ibid.
17. *Brown v. Board of Education,* 347 U.S. 483.
18. Ibid., p. 493.

19. *In re Gault*, 387, U.S. 1.
20. Ibid, p. 13.
21. *Tinker v. Des Moines School District*, 393 U.S. 503, 515.
22. *Levy v. Louisiana*, 393 U.S. 68.
23. *Tinker v. Des Moines School District*, 393 U.S. 503
24. *See 87 Harvard Law Review 1190.*
25. *See In re Pickle's Petition*, 170 So. 2d 603.
26. *In re Barker*, 2 Johns Ch. 232.
27. *In re Mason*, 1 Barb. 436.
28. *Mormon Church v. United States*, 136 U.S. 1.
29. Ibid., p.57
30. *In re Oakes*, 8 Law Rep. 112.
31. Ibid., p. 125.
32. For general discussion of this history, see 87 *Harvard Law Review 1190.*
33. *See Ford v. Ford*, 143 Mass. 577.
35. *Commonwealth v. Nickerson*, 87 Mass. 518.
35. *Rogers v. Sells*, 178 Oklahoma 103.

Chapter 3   Catastrophic Illnesses — Legal Rights

1. See Adele D. Hofman and Harriet F. Pilpel, "The Legal Rights of Children." Note 15, Chapter 2.
2. Ibid.
3. Ibid.
4. *In re Sampson*, 317 N.Y.S. 2d 641.
5. Alabama Code, Title 22 Sec. 104 (15).
6. Ibid., Sec. 104 (18).
7. Ibid., Sec. 104 (17).
8. Louisiana Revised Statutes Annotated 40-1095.
9. William Prosser, *Handbook of the Law of Torts* (St. Paul: West Publishing Co., fourth edition, 1971), p. 35.
10. *Griswold v. Connecticut*, 381 U.S. 479.
11. Ibid., p. 485.
12. *Roe v. Wade*, 410 U.S. 113; *Eisenstadt v. Baird*, 405 U.S. 483.
13. *Eisenstadt v. Baird*, 405 U.S. 483.
14. Ibid., p. 453.
15. *Roe v. Wade*, 410 U.S. 113.
16. *In re Gault*, 387 U.S. 1, 13.
17. Ibid.
18. *McKeiver v. Pennsylvania*, 403 U.S. 528.
19. *In re Gault*, 387 U.S. 28.
20. *McKeiver v. Pennsylvania*, 403 U.S. 543.
21. *Roe v. Wade*, 410 U.S. 113.
22. *Planned Parenthood of Central Mo. v. Danforth*, 428 U.S. 70.

23. Ibid., p. 74.
24. Ibid.
25 Roe v. Wade, 410U.S. 113.
26. *State v. Koome*, 84wash. 2nd 901.
27. *Planned Parenthood*, 428 U.S. 70.
28. *Carey v. Populations International Services, Inc.*, 430 U.S. 80.
29. *Roe v. Wade*, 410 U.S. 113.
30. *Planned Parenthood*, 428 U.S. 70.
31. *In re Gault*, 387 U.S. 1.
32. Ibid., p. 15
33. *Planned Parenthood*, 428 U.S. 70.
34. *Carey v. Populations International Services, Inc.*, 430 U.S. 92.
35. Ibid., p. 93.
36. *Ginsburg v. New York*, 390 U.S. 629.
37. *Prince v. Massachusetts*, 321 U.S. 158.
38. Ibid., p. 161.
39. *Carey v. Populations*, 430 U.S. 80.
40. *Ginsburg v. New York*, 390 U.S. 629.
41. *In re Gault*, 387 U.S. 1.
42. This case history is based upon a similar case observed during my research at a major cancer research hospital.
43. *Roe v. Wade*, 410 U.S. 113.
44. *Griswold v. Connecticut*, 381 U.S. 479.
45. *Planned Parenthood*, 428 U.S. 70.
46. See 83 *The Yale Law Journal* 8.
47. *Canterbury v. Spence*, 409 U.S. 1064.
48. The question of incompetency was very much at issue in the recent case of *Department of Human Services v. Northern*, 563 S.W. 2nd 197. In this case, the patient refused to allow the amputation of both of her feet — an operation believed necessary by her doctors in order to save her life. The court in directing the operation held that the patient did not comprehend the true nature of her sickness and was imcompetent. However, the court in denying Mrs. Northern the right to refuse treatment, did not overrule the *Canterbury* case, but reaffirmed the right of a competent patient to refuse life-saving treatment.
Another isolated exception to the general rule can be seen in the case of *Kennedy Memorial Hospital v. Heston*. In this case the patient, a Jehovah's Witness, refused blood transfusions necessary to save her life. In overruling the patient's right to refuse the blood transfusions, the court held that there was a compelling interest of the state to keep the patient alive since, if permitted to die, she would leave dependent children to become wards of the state. Professor Jay Katz suggests a somewhat different view in his excellent discussion of informed consent, 39 *University of Pittsburgh Law Review*, 137. I do not disagree

103

with Katz entirely, in that, the competent adult has at least the prima facie right to accept treatment or to refuse treatment. This prima facie right can under certain exceptions be overridden. However, as in the Kennedy case and other similar ones, the state must establish its compelling interest before the right can be overridden. The recent line of cases have, in the absence of a clear compelling interest of the state, reaffirmed the prima facie right of the patient to refuse medical treatment, or blood transfusions necessary to save his life. See *Palm Springs General Hospital vs. Martinez.* Civil No. 74-14-124 (C.D. Floriday January 22, 1974) *Department of Human Services vs. Northern,* 563 S.W. 2nd. 197.

49. See 83 *The Yale Law Journal* 8.
50. *In re Green,* 448 Pa. 338.
51. See 48 *So. California Law Review* 1441 for discussion of this case.
52. *In re Green,* 448 Pa. 373.
53. *In re Seiferth,* 127 N.Y.S. 2nd 63, see also 48 *Southern California Law Review* 1441, note 130.
54. *Wisconsin v. Yoder,* 406 U.S. 205.
55. Ibid, p. 242.
56. *People ex rel v. Labrenz,* 411 Ill. 618.
57. *Hoener v. Bertinato,* 67 N.J. Supp. 517. See also *Morrison v. State,* 252 S.W. 2nd 97 (blood transfusion authorized over objection of parent, a Jehovah's Witness); *In re Clark,* 90 Ohio L. Abs. 21 (where burned child might die without transfusion, treatment ordered over parent's religious beliefs); *State v. Perricone,* 37 N.J. 463, 371 U.S. 890 cert. denied (where child would die without transfusion, treatment ordered). See also *In re Vasko,* 238 App. Div. 128 (where child needed eye removed for glioma of the retina, operation ordered even though mother "would rather have her as she is now").
58. *In re Hudson,* 13 Wash. 2nd 673.
59. *In re Green,* 448 Pa. 338.
60. *In re Sampson,* 317 N.Y.S. 2nd 641 (operation ordered for facial deformity).
61. *48 So. California Law Review 1440.*
62. *In re Green,* 448 Pa. 338.
63. La. Revised Statute Annotated 40-1095.
64. *Dunham v. Wright,* 423 Fed. 2nd 940.
65. See 36 *Fordham Law Review* 639.
66. *Canterbury v. Spence,* 409 U.S. 1064.
67. Department of Health, Education and Welfare, *Guidelines,* 1973.
68. *Merriken v. Cressman,* 364 Fed. Supp. 913.
69. See Pa. Statute, Title 50, Sec. 4602; Fla. Statute 394.459 (8); Ga. Code 288-502.10; Ill. Statute, Ch. 91; Minn. Statute 246.13; Mass. General Laws, Ch. 123, Sec. 36.

70. See Alabama Code Title 22 Sec. 104 (15); La. Revised Statutes Annotated 40-1095.

Chapter 4   Catastrophic Illnesses — Ethical Rights

1. Jeremy Bentham, *Theory of Legislation* (Boston: 1840), p. 248.
2. An excellent discussion of this point is offered by Francis Schrag in his article, "This Child and the Moral Order," *Philosophy* Vol. 52 (1977). While Schrag is sympathetic to the problems connected to the separation of the two stages of childhood and adulthood, he nonetheless does not want to commit himself to any real defense of anti-paternalism insofar as children are concerned.
3. John Rawls, *A Theory of Justice* (Cambridge, Mass.: Harvard University Press, 1972).
4. Ibid., p. 5.
5. Ibid., p. 197.
6. Ibid., p. 199.
7. Ibid.
8. Ronald Dworkin, *Taking Rights Seriously* (Cambridge, Mass.: Harvard University Press, 1977), p. 181.
9. Ibid.
10. Ibid., p. 176.
11. Ibid., p. 182.
12. Ibid., p. 227.
13. Ibid., p. 200.
14. John Rawls, *A Theory of Justice*, p. 209.
15. Ibid., p. 509.
16. Although the interpretation I have placed on Rawls provides for the inclusion of a mentally defective child, Ronald Green seems to suggest in his argument for conferred rights, that Rawls does not allow for a fetus or retarded child to be included. See Ronald Green, "Conferred Rights and the Fetus," *The Journal of Religious Ethics*, Vol. 2, Spring 1974.
17. John Rawls, *A Theory of Justice*, p. 249.
18. Ronald Green, "Conferred Rights and the Fetus," p. 59.
19. John Rawls, *A Theory of Justice*, p. 250.
20. Ibid., p. 230.
21. Ibid., p. 249.
22. Some of my initial comments on Rawls are based on Victor L. Worsfold's excellent article, "A Philosophical Justification for Children's Rights," *The Rights of Children* (Cambridge, Mass.: Harvard University Press, 1974). Worsfold suggests that Rawls provides the ethical framework necessary for a philosophical justification of children's rights. Worsfold, however, discusses only the first two

conditions for any paternalistic intervention. He does not discuss the third condition as provided for by Rawls nor include Dworkin's extension of Rawls.

23. I am speaking here of rights that have been given a constituional dimension. Where these rights are based on the common law they are founded on the principle of battery

24. *Planned Parenthood of Central Mo. v. Danforth; Carey v. Populations International Services. Inc.. 428 U.S. 70.*

25. John Rawls, *A Theory of Justice*, p. 415.

26. Ibid., p. 412.

27. Ibid., p. 413.

28. Ibid., p. 415.

29. Charles Fried, *An Anatomy of Values* (Cambridge, Mass.: Harvard University Press, 1974).

30. See 83 *Yale Law Journal* 8, 1974.

31. *Natanson v. Kline*. 186 Kansas 393, p. 406.

32. *Ginsburg v. New York*. 390 U.S. 629 (in this case, the court regarded the capacity to choose as an essential condition).

33. The comments are based upon my own personal research at a major cancer research hospital where children were observed undergoing treatment for leukemia.

34. This case based upon history provided by Robert M. Veatch, *Case Studies in Medical Ethics* (Cambridge, Mass.: Harvard University Press, 1977).

35. See *Wallace v. Labrenz*, 411 I11. 618; 344 U.S. 824; *Morrison v. State*. 252 S.W. 2nd 97; *State v. Perricone*. 37 N.J. 463.

36. *Wallace v. Labrenz*. 344 U.S. 824. See also Note 48 Chapter 3, for a discussion of some exceptions to the general rule of the adult's right to consent to treatment and refuse treatment.

37. The comments are based upon my own personal research at a major cancer research hospital where children were observed undergoing treatment for leukemia.

38. Ronald Duska, *Child Studies. A Guide to Piaget and Kohlberg* (New York: Paulist Press, 1975).

39. Ibid.

40. E.A. Peel, "Intellectual Growth During Adolescence" *Readings in Child Development*. Editor, Russell C. Smart. MacMillan Company, New York 1972.

41. L. Joseph Stone and Joseph Church, *Childhood and Adolescence. A Psychology of the Growing Person* (New York: Random House, 1957).

42. *Wisconsin v. Yoder*. 406 U.S. 205.

43. Ibid, p. 231.

44. Ronald Duska, *Child Studies. A Guide to Piaget and Kohlberg; L. Joseph Stone and Joseph Church. Childhood and Adolescence. A Psychology of the Growing Person.*

45. *Taken from Robert M. Veatch, Case Studies in Medical Ethics.*
46. *This case history is based upon a similar case observed during my research at a major cancer research hospital.*
47. *This statement should not be confused with Rawls's theory of justice which is entirely contractual. The contractual element there is hypothetical, while I am specifically speaking here of contractual responsibility that is defined by law.*

Chapter 5   Mental Illnesses — Legal Rights

1. *Melville v. Sabbatino*, 30 Conn. Supp. 320.
2. Tenn. Code Annotated 33-301.
3. See 62 *Calif. Law Review* 847.
4. See *Pierce v. Society of Sisters*, 268 U.S. 510.
5. 39 *Law and Contemporary Problem* 226 (1975).
6. *Stanley v. Illinois*, 405 U.S. 645.
7. *Cleveland Board of Education v. LaFleur*, 414 U.S. 632.
8. See 62 *Calif. Law Review* 840.
9. Delaware and Texas require the child's consent for hospitalization. Del. Code 16-5123. Texas Code 5547-23. Mississippi and South Dakota do not have any provision for voluntary hospitalization and Vermont specifically excludes children from voluntary commitment provisions.
10. *In re Lee*; No. 68 (JD) 1362 (Cook County Circuit Court, Juv. Div.).
11. *Melville v. Sabbatino*, 30 Conn. Supp. 320.
12. *In re Gault*, 387 U.S. 1.
13. *Savilla v. Treadway*, Fed. Dis. Ct. Civil Action No. 6969
14. *Kremens v. Bartley*, 402 Fed. Supp. 1039.
15. *In re Gault*, 387 U.S. 1.
16. *Marsden v. Commonwealth*, 352 Mass. 564.
17. *In re Sippy*, 97 A. 2nd 455.
18. *Rouse v. Cameron*, 373 F. 2nd 451.
19. See *Griswold v. Connecticut*, 381 U.S. 479; *Roe v. Wade*, 410 U.S. 113; *Doe v. Barton*, 410 U.S. 179; and *Planned Parenthood Cases.*
20. *62 Calif. Law Review* 889.
21. *Donaldson v. O'Conner*, No. 73-1843 (5th Cir. 1974).
22. *Kaimowitz v. Dept. of Mental Health*, No. 73-19434-AW (Cir. Ct., Wayne County, Mich.).
23. See *Calif. Welfare and Institutions Code*, Sec. 5325.
24. California Code 5325 (F) (G); Ga. Code Ann. 88-502.3; Mass. General Laws Ch. 123; N.Y. Mental Hygiene Law 15.03; Washington Rev. Code 71.05; Idaho Laws 379 Ch. 838; Ore. Laws 2831; Tennessee Code Annotated 33-601.
25. Ga. Code Ann. 88-502.3 (A); N. J. Stat. Ann. 30.47.1.
26. N.Y. Mental Hygiene Law 15.03; N.C. Gen. Stat. 122.55.6.

27. See Calif. Welfare and Institutions Code 5326; Mass. Gen. Laws Ann. Ch. 123 Sec. 23.
28. Idaho Laws Ch. 173, Sec. 24.
29. *Cooper v. Roberts,* 220 Pa. Supp. 260.
30. *Canterbury v. Spence,* 409 U.S. 1064.
31. See "Informed Consent to Therapy," 64 *Northwestern Law Review* 628.
32. See *Donaldson v. O'Conner,* No. 73-1853 (5th Cir.); *Rouse v. Cameron,* 373 F. 2nd 451; *Wyatt v. Stickney,* 325 F. Supp. 781. Also 87 Harvard Law Review 1316, 1317.
33. *Jackson v. Indiana,* 406 U.S. 715; *In re Davis,* 8 Calif. 3rd 798.
34. *Wyatt v. Stickney,* 325 F. Supp. 781.
35. Ibid., p. 785.
36. *Donaldson v. O'Conner,* No. 73-1843 (5th Cir.).
37. Ibid., p. 3152.

38. *Eisenstadt v. Baird,* 405 U.S. 483.
39. *Wyatt v. Stickney,* 325 F. Supp. 785.
40. Ibid., 334 F. Supp. 1343.
41. For discussion of *Stickney* case, see 87 *Harvard Law Review* 1338.
42. *Logan v. United States,* 144 U.S. 263.
43. 87 *Harvard Law Review* 1364.
44. *Jobson v. Hume,* 355 Fed. 2nd 129.
45. See *Taylor v. Georgia,* 315 U.S. 25.
46. *Jobson v. Hume,* 355 Fed. 2d 129.
47. *Wyatt v. Stickney,* 325 F. Supp. 781.
48. A. Louis McGarry and Honora A. Kaplan, "Trends in Mental Health Law," *American Journal of Psychiatry* 130:6 June 1973.
49. Ibid., p. 628.
50. *In re Lifschutz,* 356 F. 2nd 82.

Chapter 6   Mental Illnesses — Ethical Rights

1. Thomas Szasz, *The Myth of Mental Illness* (New York: Basic Books, 1965).
2. See 83 *Yale Law Journal* 8.
3. See 62 *California Law Review* 1025.
4 The presumption of the loss of rationality should not be confused with the "presumption of rationality" which I have employed throughout my essay. Legally, once a court has made a determination that there is a loss of rationality the burden shifts to the patient to overcome a continuing presumption of the loss of rationality. The patient must re-establish his rationality by overcoming the presumption.
5. Cynthia's case history is based upon similar cases studied during my research at a major state psychiatric hospital.

6. See 87 *Harvard Law Review* 1412 and J. Page, "The Science of Understanding Deviance," *Psychopathology* 32-55: 1971.
7. *Kelly v. Davis*, 216 Ark. 828.
8. Ibid., p. 835.
9. *In re Stephen's Will*, 294 N.Y.S. 624.
10. *United States v. Adams*, 297 Fed. Supp. 596.
11. See 87 *Harvard Law Review* 1215, note 81.
12. See 87 *Harvard Law Review* 1216, note 84.
13. See 47 *So. California Law Review* 308.
14. See Note 42, Chapter 4.
15. See *In re Gault*, 387 U.S. 1.
16. Thomas Szasz, *The Myth of Mental Illness.*
17. *See Florida Statutes 394.459; Georgia Code 88-502.19; Ill. Statutes Ch. 91; California Welfare and Institution Code 5350.*
18. *See 62 California Law Review 1974.*
19. Thomas Scheff, "Being Mentally Ill," *Sociological Theory,* 171, 1966.
20. See note 5.
21. See 62 *California Law Review* 861.
22. R. D. Laing, "Intervention in Social Situations," *The Politics of the Family and Other Essays,* 33:1971.

BIBLIOGRAPHY

Books

Adams, Paul (ed.). *Children's Rights Toward the Liberation of the Child.* New York: Praeger Publishers, 1971.

Aries, Philippe. *Centuries of Childhood.* New York: Alfred A. Knapf, 1962.

Bentham, Jeremy. *Theory of Legislation.* Boston, 1840.

Berger, Nan. "The Child, the Law, and the State," *Toward the Liberation of the Child,* ed. Paul Adams. New York: Praeger Publishers, 1971.

Drinin, Robert F. "The Rights of Children in Modern American Family Law," *The Rights of Children: Emergent Concepts in Law and Society,* ed. by Albert E. Wilkerson. Temple University Press, 1973.

Duska, Ronald. *Child Studies, A Guide to Piaget and Kohlberg.* New York: Paulist Press, 1975.

Dworkin, Ronald. *Taking Rights Seriously.* Cambridge: Mass.: Harvard University Press, 1977.

Farson, Richard. *Birthrights.* New York: MacMillan Publishing Company, 1974.

Fried, Charles. *An Anatomy of Values.* Cambridge, Mass.: Harvard University Press, 1974.

Hobbes, Thomas. *Leviathan.* London: J. Bohn, 1839. Molesworth ed.

Locke, John. *The Second Treatise of Government.* New York: Bobbs-Merrill, 1952.

Melden, A.I. *Rights and Right Conduct.* Oxford: Basil Blackwell, 1959.

Mill, John Stuart. *On Liberty.* New York: Washington Square Press, 1963.

Prosser, William. *Handbook of the Law of Torts.* St. Paul: West Publishing Co., fourth edition, 1971.

Rawls, John. *A Theory of Justice.* Cambridge, Mass.: Harvard University Press, 1972.

Szasz, Thomas. *The Myth of Mental Illness.* New York: Basic Books, 1965.

Veatch, Robert M. *Case Studies in Medical Ettics.* Cambridge, Mass.: Harvard University Press, 1977.

Worsfold, Victor L. "A Philosophical Justification for Children's Rights," *The Rights of Children, Harvard Educational Review.* Cambridge, Mass.: Harvard University Press, 1974.

Articles

62 *California Law Review* 847.

"Constitutional Right of Privacy," 48 *Southern California Law Review* 1441.

Department of Health, Education and Welfare, *Guidelines*, 1973.

"Development-Civil Commitment," 87 *Harvard Law Review* **1190.**

Feinberg, Joel. "The Nature and Value of Rights," *The Journal of Value Enquiry*, Vol. 4 (1970) 243-257.

Green, Ronald. "Conferred Rights and the Fetus," *The Journal of Religious Ethics*, Vol. 2, Spring 1974.

Hofman, Adele D. and Pilpel, Harriet F. "The Legal Rights of Minors," *The Pediatric Clinics of North America* 20:989.

"Informed Consent," 36 *Fordham Law Review* 630.

"Informed Consent and the Dying Patient," 83 *Yale Law Journal* 8.

"Informed Consent to Therapy," 64 *Northwestern Law Review* 628.

Katz, Jay. "Informed Consent," 39 *University of Pittsburgh Law Review* 137.

Laing, R.D. "Intervention in Social Situations," *The Politics of the Family and Other Essays*, 33:1971.

39 *Law and Contemporary Problems* 226, 1975.

McGarry, A. Louis and Kaplan, Honora A. "Trends in Mental Health Law," *American Journal of Psychiatry* 130:6, June 1973.

Miami Symposium on the Prediction of Behavior. "Use of Aversive Stimulation in Behavior Modification," *Aversive Stimulation*, Jones Edition, 1968.

Page, J. "The Science of Understanding Deviance," *Psycholopathology*, 1971.

Scheff, Thomas. "Being Mentally Ill," *Socialogical Theory*, 171, 1966.

Wasserstrom, Richard. "Rights, Human Rights, and Racial Discrimination," *Journal of Philosophy*, Vol. 61, 1964.

Law Cases

Brown v. Board of Education, 347 U.S. 483.

Canterbury v. Spence, 409 U.S. 1064.

Carey v. Populations International Services, Inc., 430 U.S. 80.

Cleveland Board of Education v. LaFleur, 414 U.S. 632.

Commonwealth v. Nickerson, 87 Mass. 518.

Cooper v. Roberts, 220 Pa. Supp. 260.

Doe v. Barton, 410 U.S. 179.

Donaldson v. O'Conner, No. 73-1843 (5th Cir. 1974).

Dunham v. Wright, 423 Fed. 2nd 940.

Eisenstadt v. Baird, 405 U.S. 483.

Ford v. Ford, 143 Mass. 577.

Ginsburg v. New York, 390 U.S. 629.

Griswold v. Connecticut, 381 U.S. 479.

Hoener v. Bertinato, 67 N.J. Supp. 517.

In re Barker, 2 Johns Ch. 232.

In re Clark, 50 Ohio Law Abstracts 21.

In re Davis, 8 Calif. 3rd 798.

In re Gault, 387 U.S. 1.

In re Green, 448 Pa. 338.

In re Hudson, 13 Wash. 2nd 673.

In re Lee, No. 68 (JD) 1362 (Cook County, Cir. Ct. J. Div.).

In re Lifschutz, 356 F. 2nd 82.

In re Mason, 1 Barb. 436.

In re Oakes, 8 Law Reports 112.

In re Pickle's Petition, 170 So. 2nd 603.

In re Sampson, 317 N.Y.S. 2nd 641.

In re Seiferth, 127 N.Y.S. 2nd 63.

In re Sippy, 97 A. 2nd 455.

In re Stephen's Will, 294 N.Y.S. 624.

In re Vasko, 238 App. Div. 128.

Jackson v. Indiana, 406 U.S. 715.

Jobson v. Hume, 355 Fed. 2nd 129.

Kaimowitz v. Dept. of Mental Health, No. 73-19434-AW (Cir. Ct., Wayne County, Mich.).

Kelly v. Davis, 216 Ark. 828.

Kremens v. Bartley, 402 Fed. Supp. 1039.

Levy v. Louisiana, 391 U.S. 68.

Logan v. United States, 144 U.S. 263.

Marsden v. Commonwealth, 352 Mass. 564.

McKeiver v. Pennsylvania, 403 U.S. 528.

Melville v. Sabbatino, 30 Conn. Supp. 320.

Merriken v. Cressman, 364 Fed. Supp. 913.

Mormon Church v. United States, 136 U.S. 1.

Morrison v. State, 252 Southwestern 2nd 97.

Natanson v. Kline, 186 Kansas 393.

People ex rel v. Labrenz, 411 Ill. 618.

Pierce v. Society of Sisters, 268 U.S. 510.

Planned Parenthood of Central Mo. v. Danforth, 428 U.S. 70.

Prince v. Massachusetts, 321 U.S. 158.

Roe v. Wade, 410 U.S. 113.

Rogers v. Sells, 178 Oklahoma 103.

Rouse v. Cameron, 373 Fed. 2nd 451.

Saville v. Treadway, Fed. Dis. Ct. Civil Action No. 6969.

Stanley v. Illinois, 405 U.S. 645.

State v. Koome, 84 Wash. 2nd 901.

State v. Perricone, 37 N.J. 463.

Taylor v. Georgia, 315 U.S. 25

Tinker v. Des Moines School District, 393 U.S. 503.

United States v. Adams, 297 Fed. Supp. 596

United States v. Orito, 413 U.S. 139.

Wallace v. Labrenz, 411 Ill. 618.

Wisconsin v. Yoder, 406 U.S. 205.

Wyatt v. Stickney, 325 Fed. Supp. 781.

State Statutes

Alabama Code Title 22 Sec. 104.

California Welfare and Institutions Code Section 5325.

Delaware Code 16-5123

Florida Statutes 394.459 (8).

Georgia Code Section 88.502.10.

Idaho Laws Chapter 173 Sec. 24; Chapter 379 Sec. 838.

Ill. Statutes Chapter 91.

Louisiana Revised Statutes Annotated 40-1095.

Mass. General Laws, Chapter 123, Sec. 36.

Minn. Statutes 246.13.

New Jersey Mental Hygiene Laws 15.03.

North Carolina Statutes 122-55.6.

Pennsylvania Statutes Title 50, Sec. 4602.

Tennessee Code Annotated 33-301.

Texas Code 5547-23.

Washington Revised Code 71.05.

Index

Voluntary Commitment
  distinction from involuntary, 89

Work Notes, 96
Wisconsin v. Yoder, 74
Wyatt v. Stickley, 74-76

ABOUT THE AUTHOR

Frank H. Marsh is an Associate Professor of Philosophy at Old Dominion University. After undergraduate and graduate preparation in law, he practiced as a trial lawyer for twenty-three years. He then turned to the study of medical ethics, in which he received his Ph.D. degree from the University of Tennessee. He is a frequent contributor to professional journals.